REMEMBERING THE FUTURE

REMEMBERING THE FUTURE

Vatican II and Tomorrow's Liturgical Agenda

edited by
Carl A. Last

paulist press  new york/ramsey

Acknowledgements
The Publisher gratefully acknowledges the use of excerpts from *The Jerusalem Bible,* copyright © 1966 by Darton, Longman & Todd, Ltd. and Doubleday & Company, Inc. Reprinted by permission of the publisher. All rights reserved.

Library of Congress
Catalog Card Number: 83-62469

ISBN: 0-8091-2562-5

Published by Paulist Press
545 Island Road, Ramsey, N.J. 07446

Printed and bound in the
United States of America

Contents

Foreword

Most Reverend Rembert G. Weakland, O.S.B.,
Archbishop of Milwaukee

So often, when we have worked for long hours and through many meetings on a document, we feel our work is done. The contrary is usually true. The document must then be taught and become a part of the thinking of those who are to implement it. Unfortunately, so many aspects of the documents of the Second Vatican Council have been neglected or have not become our own because of the lack of thorough education and implementation. Sometimes only vague and general concepts about the documents remain in the minds of the faithful.

One of the advantages of celebrating the twentieth anniversary of the Second Vatican Council and its documents is that it gives us all the occasion again to study more in depth what is in those important documents. It gives us a new and privileged occasion to read them again and to study them more intensely. We also have the advantage of distance and a few decades of experience. When these documents were first published, there were so many of them that one could not keep up with the full meaning of their message. Now we can take our study more slowly and treat each document more completely.

Perhaps there is no document which requires so much study and reflection as the very first one on the liturgy—*Sacrosanctum Concilium.* Many have observed that it would have been more prudent to have begun with a different subject and to have saved the theme of liturgy to the very end. There is much truth in that observation, but it is too late now to reverse history. Probably, too, many European nations were more ready for the liturgical changes than we were here in the United States. There had been a strong liturgical revival in our country, but it was still peripheral and had not yet reached the larger part of the Catholic population and had not yet been taught in the seminaries and become a part of priestly formation. Our training had been, for the most part, very rubrical and exact. We were not ready for the thorough and complete rethinking that was demanded by the Vatican II decrees.

Much has happened in the meantime. We all are aware of the intense controversies about liturgy which have filled the Church atmosphere since then. I leave aside the bizarre criticisms which I have found mostly in the American Catholic integrist press about the implementation of the document being in the hands of Protestants and other similar absurdities. Having been a member of the *Consilium ad exequendum*, I know how much of this kind of unfounded untruth has also surrounded the liturgical renewal effort. All of that must be left aside and the real questions and issues faced, questions which are so important for the spiritual life of the Church.

In addition to this general study of the document again and the need to acquaint ourselves with its contents and its theology in the light of the events which led up to it, we must also see its implications for the inner spiritual life of the Church today. After two decades or more we still must be concerned about all of those misunderstandings and obstacles which prevent its full implementation. Perhaps among these the most important are the insights which the social sciences have had to offer about changes in liturgy and worship that affect the Catholic identity. These problems are of special importance in those cases where the changes have been only exterior and were not accompanied by inner convictions and persuasions.

For all of these reasons, I am sure that essays as those found in this collection will aid all of us in becoming better acquainted with the document on liturgy itself, with its inner logic and meaning, with its intent, and, most of all, with the spiritual thrust which it hopes to engender in the Church. Perhaps in this way many of the *lacunae* in our educative process twenty-some years ago can be closed now and done so with more insight and experience than would have been available to us then.

Introduction

Carl A. Last

I was ordained in 1969. The Second Vatican Council had ended just a few years earlier and the effects of the promulgation of the *Constitution on the Sacred Liturgy* were just beginning to be felt in parishes. The quote from the Book of Revelation, "Behold, I make all things new," seemed an appropriate motto for my ordination and first Mass invitations and prayer cards. I was filled with excitement and enthusiasm over the possibilities for the Church's renewal that lay ahead and was more than impressed that, at this moment in the Church's history, I had been called to the service of leadership. Admittedly, in my wide-eyed enthusiasm, I was not prepared for the anxieties, frustrations, disappointments and sometimes open conflict that seemingly sudden and dramatic change brought to the people I was called to serve.

This bit of "remembrance" was forcefully brought to mind recently as I paged through my ordination photo album with my teenaged nephews and nieces. I became painfully aware that the ecclesial and liturgical vision captured for all time through the eye of a camera was a part of the past with which young people of today have little, if any, experience and understanding. Their giggles at an overly ornate church, their comments about my "Infant of Prague-like" vesture and the "old guy" (my pastor who insisted on being arch-priest) looking over my shoulder as well as the "maleness" of the occasion helped me to realize how rooted the reform liturgy of Pope Paul VI has become.

I dare say that for most Catholics today, liturgical experiences and expressions of the decades before the Council are rather remote—often nostalgic childhood recollections. For these same people, the liturgical apostolate—those people, events and forces that led to the 1963 conciliar debate and its decisions about Christian worship—are largely unknown, or, at best, footnotes in history.

While we can applaud the successes of the liturgical reform movement initiated for the universal Church with the promulgation of the *Constitution on the Sacred Liturgy*, we might also be aware that those successes can be short-circuited and the full vision of *Sacrosanctum Concilium* largely unrealized. The task before us as we move into the third decade of liturgical reform, "our future agenda," depends on an understanding of our preconciliar history—those developments which served as a vitally important context for the liturgy document. It depends also on our deepening awareness of the theological content of the Constitution and its impact on post-conciliar documentation and developments. It depends, finally, upon the assimilation in our own time and culture of one of the major points of magisterial teaching: the role of liturgy as central to all the Church's activity and the embodiment of the great "Mysterium Fidei" as the source of our spiritual life.

This collection of papers, published in celebration of the twentieth anniversary of the promulgation of *Sacrosanctum Concilium*, December 4, 1963, is presented as a humble contribution to individuals and church communities as we face the challenges of tomorrow's liturgical agenda. They originated out of a determination in the church of Milwaukee to celebrate the achievements of the Second Vatican Council with a special commemorative series on the major themes and documents of that historic and Spirit-filled event. Happily, our first topic, simply entitled "Celebrating Vatican II: The Liturgy," was a study of the *Constitution on the Sacred Liturgy*, not only because it was the first work completed by the Council, but also because, in the words of Pope Paul VI, "the liturgy was the first subject to be examined and the first too, in a sense, in intrinsic worth and in importance for the life of the Church."

The five chapters which follow aid us as we attempt to

remember into the future. We begin by highlighting those persons and groups involved in the decades preceding the Council and how they and the events of that period contributed to and shaped the textual development of *Sacrosanctum Concilium.* Primary among those influences are the Church's official embrace of the liturgical movement itself, the liturgical scholarship of the period as well as a return to the sources which revealed a sound doctrine of liturgy. These gave legitimacy to change while preserving continuity and organic growth. However, not to be underestimated are the widespread popular and even pragmatic influences which made a significant pastoral contribution. These influences, as well as those of other movements in the Church (biblical, catechetical, ecumenical, etc.), illustrate that *Sacrosanctum Concilium* did not appear suddenly and full blown but grew out of a profound movement within the Church community, a sign of the continuing activity of God's Spirit in the Church.

A second chapter provides us with a critical examination of *Sacrosanctum Concilium,* including a brief comparison between the reform of Trent and that of Vatican II, showing some striking similarities but also basic differences between the approaches of these two Councils. It demonstrates that the pastoral orientation of the Constitution derives from the theology of the liturgy and is understandable only in light of that theology. The heart of that theology, of course, is the paschal mystery of Jesus as the origin, foundation and goal of the Church. Liturgy, therefore, is not simply the place where Christians obtain spiritual nourishment. As the co-working of Christ and the Church, it is the activity "par excellence" in which the holy people is concretely manifested and realized, growing into the fullness of Christ by continually dying and rising, through, with and in him.

An overview of post-conciliar documentation and legislation provides readers with a necessary bridge. The whole process of liturgical reform has been fraught with anxiety and polarization from which the Church still suffers. This confusion which has been magnified by extensive cultural developments and pluralism throughout the world is further compounded by the failure of leadership and the significant lack of conviction on all levels about the centrality of liturgy in the Christian Economy.

Therefore, a final stage of liturgical reform is called for by *Sacrosanctum Concilium*, especially nn. 37–40 (but always in light of other articles and sections): liturgical indigenization and cultural adaptation of the Roman rituals, as the surest way of promoting a genuine liturgical life in local churches throughout the world. It is suggested that as long as the liturgy is untouched by the cultures of the people, it will remain alien, and the mystery it bears will penetrate the depths of our hearts only with the greatest difficulty.

The challenge for the future, then, is the development of what might be called a liturgical spirituality: that overall orientation of our lives grounded upon the revelation of God in the human community. The authentic liturgical life of the community of faith is a key factor in our journey toward the fullness of human existence. This "Mysterium Fidei" shocks our world view. Our sovereign God is Emmanuel, inseparably bound to this world of broken flesh through the Spirit of Jesus dwelling in us. We discover this mystery, and ourselves, in the breaking of the bread.

> The liturgy daily builds up those who are in the Church, making them a holy temple of the Lord, a dwelling place for God in the Spirit, to the mature measure of the fullness of Christ (SC 2).

I wish to express my deep appreciation to the authors of this collection for sharing their faith and the fruit of their own scholarship with the people of Milwaukee through their participation in last fall's conference, "Celebrating Vatican II." I wish to thank them for agreeing to share their papers with a wider audience through this publication. Their additional devoted labor places me more firmly, with admiration, friendship and respect, in their debt.

I wish also to express my gratitude to Archbishop Rembert

Weakland, O.S.B., pastor of the Church of Milwaukee, for his leadership, commitment and support, and to the community of St. Francis Seminary and the staff of the Albert Cardinal Meyer Institute for their encouragement and patience.

1
The Sacred Liturgy: Tradition and Change

Frederick R. McManus

To describe the context and the process of the 1963 *Constitution on the Sacred Liturgy, Sacrosanctum Concilium*, with particular emphasis upon the American experience, is partly an exercise in nostalgia, partly a necessary introduction to the first of the conciliar documents. In some ways it was the document most striking and pervasive in its effects; in any event it was one of the most significant of the Council's decrees.

In telling the story of the Constitution, including its context in the decade before the convocation of the Second Vatican Council, the name of Archbishop Annibale Bugnini will always be a major part of the background.[1] He was a great priest and liturgist whom the providence of God placed in the Church at a critical moment. After thorough academic preparation and a university teaching career, Bugnini served the Liturgical Commission of Pope Pius XII set up in 1948, the Preparatory Commission on the Liturgy of 1960–1962, the Consilium for the Implementation of the Constitution on the Liturgy named in 1964, and the Congregation for Divine Worship from 1969 until 1975. His final service to the Church Community, as pro-nuncio in Iran from 1976 until his sudden death in 1982, so alien to his other responsibilities and for which he was so slightly prepared, may be the greatest crown in his accomplishments. In those most difficult circumstances, with nothing but personal humiliation as a likely reward, he displayed the most profound Christian charity and courage.

Bruce Laingen, the senior foreign service officer among the American hostages during their crisis in Iran, wrote about him: "The human spirit has lost one of its strongest champions in the death of Archbishop Annibale Bugnini in Rome. As papal nuncio in Tehran during the hostage crisis, he was constant in his concern and unceasing in his prayers for the hostages, whom he described in a letter to me as his 'colleagues of solitude.' He felt deeply and personally our loss of freedom and our separation from families. None of us will forget his visits at Christmas and Easter, his gentle and unassuming personality, his confidence in our eventual release. Annibale Bugnini was a true man of God."[2]

But it is of course Bugnini's liturgical accomplishments which we here record and praise. He was quite literally the chief architect of the liturgical reform—from 1948 until 1975. In particular, during the first two years of the Second Vatican Council (1962–1963), as *peritus* of the conciliar commission, he contributed to the revision of the *Constitution on the Sacred Liturgy* and began planning its implementation with Pope Paul VI and Cardinal Giacomo Lercaro of Bologna.[3] Throughout these many years of his involvement, in spite of every conceivable obstacle from within a Roman curia that was basically unfriendly to liturgical reform and of every conceivable and sometimes ludicrous vilification from outside,[4] Bugnini displayed pastoral sense, fidelity to the Council's mandate, respect for the traditions of the Roman liturgy, and openness to the working of the Spirit of God discerned in the life of the Christian people.

It is for others in this collection to evaluate the successes and failures of the Council's liturgical initiatives, but I must begin by asserting unequivocally that any of the limitations, weaknesses or compromises, even the so-called excesses, are small and slight by comparison with the achievement and the progress. Let me use a single sentence from a recent article by James Tunstead Burtchaell to sum up what has happened in the course of the two decades since the conciliar fathers debated the draft of the *Constitution on the Sacred Liturgy* in the fall of 1962: "The sacraments are in a tongue unloosed now, and can be celebrated with an imagination and an integrity that release more of their grace and power than before."[5]

The Pre-Conciliar Context

It is difficult to appreciate how remote their liturgical experiences of the 1940's and 1950's are for the majority of Catholic believers today. This is equally true of the liturgical apostolate and of the forces that led, with excruciating gradualness, to the 1962 conciliar debate and decision on Christian worship.

Therefore, these pages will trace, in summary and simplified form, the several threads that made up the fabric to be woven by the Council, beginning with the official (and perhaps less important) context, moving on in succession to the scholarly situation of the decade or so before the Council, then to the pastoral movement, and finally to the contextual relationships of other movements of the Spirit within the Church. All this will be done in the light of the American liturgical enterprise of the 1940's and 1950's.

The Contribution of the Liturgical Movement

Slightly more than a decade before Pope John suddenly announced his plan for a general council, Pope Pius XII had literally adopted the liturgical movement in his 1947 encyclical letter *Mediator Dei* on the public worship of the Church.[6] This document, still worthy of study and reflection, was the fruit of the chant, monastic, scholarly, theological, and social dimensions of the nineteenth and twentieth century liturgical movements. Influenced especially by popular developments in France, Belgium, Germany, and Austria, the encyclical is now much dated; even then it was very cautionary in tone. It was nonetheless the charter of the liturgical apostolate in the late 1940's and the 1950's.

This encyclical was also an implicit acknowledgement that

the revision and reform efforts under Pope Pius X at the beginning of the century had to be resumed—efforts to purge the Roman liturgy of undesirable accretions and, more positively, to revitalize the liturgy as the work and deed of a praying community of believers.

This latter dimension of reform is much less evident from the encyclical itself than from what followed, quietly and unnoticeably, in the next year, when a commission of liturgical restoration—always a euphemism for reform—was set up. The scope of this commission was broad enough. Its accomplishments were substantial: the Easter Vigil restoration of 1951, the Holy Week reform of 1955, an initial simplification of rubrics and partial pruning of the Church Calendar, the first stages in the revision of the Roman Pontifical and the Rites of Christian Initiation. It is an impressive list of contributions made up to the very opening of the Second Vatican Council. But this period was also marked officially by the first real although hesitant breakdown in the resistance to vernacular developments—the several bi-lingual rituals. An equally important development was the grudging concession of the dialogue Mass and of vernacular song at, but not an "official" part of, the recited liturgy. These were a revolution in the 1950's, although they look like meager, paltry concessions as we now look back over thirty years and more.

Since this review should be one of persons as well as of events and movements, at least the chief curial participants in the pre-conciliar liturgical reform need to be mentioned. One was the Franciscan Ferdinando Antonelli, later secretary of the Conciliar Commission on the Liturgy. In the 1950's he headed the historical section of the venerable Congregation of Rites, to which, in 1930, Pope Pius XI had entrusted the historical study needed for the revision of the official liturgical books. Better attuned to pastoral-liturgical needs was his associate, the Redemptionist Josef Loew, who did not live to see the fruits of his efforts during the Council. And, in 1948, the young Vincentian Annibale Bugnini, as the commission's secretary, began his lengthy official participation in the process that preceded the Council.

The continuity of the pre-conciliar process is suggested by the language with which John XXIII introduced the new code of rubrics for the Mass and the Divine Office in 1960.[7] He acknowledged the still unfinished work of the commission set up by his predecessor and proposed that the broad lines of renewal and reform should be determined by the forthcoming Council. It was at this time that the overall goals of the Council and the influence of the pre-conciliar commission were becoming clear, the lines that are admirably summed up in the opening paragraph of the *Constitution on the Sacred Liturgy*. They deserve paraphrasing even now: *to strengthen the Christian life of believers, to accommodate church institutions to contemporary needs, to promote unity among Christians, and to call all of humankind into the family of the Church.*

The Influence of Liturgical Scholarship

A second thread or strain from the period immediately before the Council, but of course long antedating it, is the scholarly research into the traditions of the Roman and other liturgies of the Chrisian churches, a research which ran parallel to other scholarly movements of the time and was characterized during the Council as a "return to the sources." Because those who were to write the drafts and rewrite the conciliar schema on the liturgy were deeply immersed in this scholarship, its contribution needs a word of explanation.

The charge of archaeologism in liturgical reform is not only poorly nuanced, it is actually false. No responsible scholar could propose the impossible restoration of a third, fifth, seventh, or ninth century liturgy. Instead, what was at issue, both before and during the Council, was precedent, continuity and organic growth. Above all, only a sound knowledge of the diverse liturgical traditions permits selectivity in the light of contemporary situations. Liturgical scholarship revealed to the Council a sounder doctrine of the liturgy and, importantly, gave legitimacy to further change.

A comparison with the post-Tridentine liturgical reform is worthwhile. To us the notion of reviving a pristine or patristic liturgy seems naive; we can easily say it is both undesirable and impossible. Yet that was the intent of the reformers under Pope Pius V.[8] What scholarship does achieve is a sense that it "was not always so," a realization of the contingent and conditional nature of most ritual and textual elements that go to make up any one of the Christian liturgies, whether Roman or Mozarabic, Byzantine or Maronite.

In the next section the relationship of scholars to the pastoral specialists in the decade before the Council will be more evident. Here a note is needed on the rather limited instances of American liturgical scholarship. This is often and rightly called derivative, because the names of original research scholars are few. Most American writers were largely dependent upon European studies. However, among the great scholars in the U.S. was Johannes Quasten of The Catholic University of America who guided patristic and liturgical research at that institution during the period before the Council. He was a member of the Preparatory Commission on the Liturgy, as was Godfrey Diekmann, O.S.B. of Collegeville—the continuator of Virgil Michel, O.S.B. Dom Virgil, like Dom Godfrey, represented the happy combination of liturgical scholarship with broader social and ecclesial concerns. Another of the relatively few Americans with strong scholarly credentials in liturgical studies was Gerald Ellard, S.J.; he was also a popularizer by means of his college textbooks and, to a greater extent than the others, a strong prophet of liturgical reform as such.

A word needs to be added about the advanced academic programs in the United States in the period immediately preceding the Council. Again these programs would be characterized, without any suggestion of reproach or criticism, as somewhat derivative.

There is a contrast between the University of Notre Dame and The Catholic University of America in this regard. In the former, the decade before the Council saw a major development through the initiatives of a single priest, himself a missionary rather than a research scholar, Michael Mathis of the Holy Cross Fathers. The graduate program which he began, at first at the master's level, later with a strong research track, and finally a distinctive and successful Ph.D. program, took advantage of European visiting scholars as well as Americans. Its success, even in the period before the Council, can hardly be overestimated, although its quantitative results were limited, like the rest of the preconciliar liturgical movement. At Catholic University, on the other hand, the substantial liturgical contributions along scholarly lines were in the Ph.D. and S.T.D. programs in a diversity of departments: theology, religion, patristic Greek and Latin. It was only after the Council that a master's level program in formally distinct liturgical studies was introduced.

The Pastoral Contribution

Overlapping the scholarly context was the pastoral development, then variously called the liturgical apostolate or liturgical movement. This third strain was practical, even pragmatic, and it was intended to be popular. But no overview of it is correct unless it is understood as very limited in the numbers of persons and parishes affected.

The liturgical movement of the late 1940's and 1950's—and even more the earlier liturgical renewal—could be characterized as sound, pastoral, spiritually oriented, authentically ecclesial, and all the rest. But it was not widespread in its influence upon the sacramental life of the ordinary parish or community. Reading the Catholic press, papers, and magazines of the period prior to the Council, and especially reading the journals addressed to a clerical audience, one would see relatively little reference to liturgical renewal or lay participation. Even the official developments already mentioned were generally treated with reserve or indifference.

Nonetheless the depth and insights of the popular dimensions of the liturgical movement can hardly be overestimated. These in turn gave rise, in the late 1960's and later, to the myth that liturgical revision was the work of a few very influential (and perhaps malign) persons. Unhappily this faulty view did not, it seems, lead to the conclusion that such reform-minded persons, who were not few but many, were correct in their judgments or were signs of the movement of the Holy Spirit in the Church, to use the words of Pius XII taken up in the Constitution on the *Sacred Liturgy.*[9]

A choice between the two strongest American forces in this pastoral context is difficult. Both the Liturgical Weeks (dating back to 1940 under the sponsorship of the Benedictine Liturgical Conference and to 1943 under the sponsorship of The Liturgical Conference) and the journal *Orate, Fratres* (now *Worship*) deserve equal treatment.

The Liturgical Weeks were national in scope and indeed international because of strong Canadian participation. The diversity of their themes and the substance of the formal presentations which preceded the discussions demonstrate the direction of the liturgical movement for formation or education and improved liturgical celebration. The Liturgical Weeks, in their published (and invaluable) annual *Proceedings,*[10] are less revealing about issues of liturgical revision and reform, although such issues frequently surfaced in very measured terms.

The promoters of liturgical renewal were reformers and prophets at heart, but only secondarily so. It is an illusion, understandable in the light of the great reforms that were to come, that The Liturgical Conference was primarily concerned with reworking the Order of Mass or the ritual of the sacraments. The Conference and its Liturgical Weeks can be better characterized as concerned with improving things as they were, with finding means to celebrate well and authentically within the restricted forms of the Roman rite. That this limitation compounded the difficulties of the task need not be stressed.

Perhaps the best evidence of this approach was the determined effort of The Liturgical Conference, as it planned the annual Weeks, to keep at arm's length the Vernacular Society, a body which generally met at the same time and in the same place. By and large the members of the Conference and the participants in the Liturgical Weeks were completely convinced of the need to return to a vernacular liturgy. Yet prudential and political reasons kept this significant issue from any great prominence in the formal discussions of the Weeks themselves. Instead primacy was rightly given to the best forms and styles in which to celebrate the unreformed Roman liturgy in Latin and to the true meaning of the signs and symbols which manifest the common prayer of the Christian assembly.

The diversity of themes of the Liturgical Weeks stands now as an indication of the depth and foresight of these congresses. The themes, and especially the individual papers, give the lie to later prophetic voices which speak of novel discoveries in the post-conciliar period as if there were no prologue to our present liturgical concerns. A selection of these, for the decade or so before the calling and convening of the Council, will illustrate this point: *The Family in Christ* (1946), *The New Man in Christ* (Christian Initiation, 1948), *Sanctification of Sunday* (1949), *The Priesthood of Christ* (1951), *Saint Pius X and Social Worship* (1953), *Liturgy and Social Order* (1955), *People's Participation and Holy Week* (1956), *Education and the Liturgy* (1957), *The Liturgy and Unity in Christ* (liturgical dimensions of ecumenism, 1960). Even as the conciliar process was going on, the same breadth was evident: *Bible, Life, and Worship* (1961), *Thy Kingdom Come: Christian Hope in the Modern World* (1962), *Jesus Christ Reforms His Church* (1963).

The papers given at the Liturgical Weeks were not the profound results of original scholarly research, but they were produced after wide reading in the secondary sources, reflection upon the pastoral scene by pastoral specialists, and thorough acquaintance with the biblical and liturgical sources. But the flavor of the presentations and the discussions cannot be grasped without mention of a still more important element: the Liturgical Weeks were much more successful as spiritual retreats, as times of prayer and reflection and celebration, than most of the retreats of the period, certainly much more than the traditional parish missions. And the more serious academic side was a concern as well, especially with the introduction of theological and biblical meetings preceding the more popular programs of the Weeks themselves. The only problem was that all the participants in the Weeks understandably wanted to be included in the specialized sessions as well.

The length of this summary, in comparison with what may and should be said about *Orate, Fratres,* is not to minimize the latter but only to recognize that, as *Worship,* the journal remains familiar to today's audience of liturgical promoters and its volumes are readily accessible in libraries. It has become the indispensable journal, serious and scholarly as well as pastoral in its concerns, for liturgists and liturgiologists alike, and without equal in any language. From its establishment in the mid-twenties, *Orate, Fratres* combined the popular and pastoral with articles reflecting the best of European scholarship. Its successive editors, first Virgil Michel, who was both liturgist and sociologist, then Godfrey Diekmann, both scholar and popularizer—and principal influence upon the American movement in the period before the Council—managed to find a balance between popular and scholarly.

A thorough study of the growth and impact of *Orate, Fratres,* as well as of the Liturgical Weeks before the Council, needs to be done. This is not the place to enumerate the major contributors. Two names only may be mentioned, both prominent in the Liturgical Weeks as well as in *Orate, Fratres:* Martin Hellriegel was the ideal liturgical pastor of the period, inventive, creative, deeply spiritual, well read and reflective.[11] Hans Reinhold was the effervescent interpreter of all things liturgical, but always in the broadest ecclesial and social context.[12] He was a fierce combatant in the liturgical wars, but personally a simple and humble and shy Christian.

The concentration here has been on the American scene, and intentionally so. But this is an incomplete treatment, partly because of the doubtless greater influence of the European liturgical movements upon what was to come in the Second Vatican Council.

The research scholarship has already been mentioned. There is no need to return, beyond our period of consideration, to the great monastic and chant influences of Solesmes and Maria Laach. It might be pointed out, however, that earlier pioneers and certainly the great Lambert Beaudouin situated the liturgical movement squarely in the midst of popular and social movements in the Church, far removed from the merely monastic scene or the alleged ivory and aesthetic tower.

Much space could be devoted to persons, places, and events,

such as the centers or institutes which grew up in Paris and Trier after the Second World War and which were committed to pastoral liturgy or liturgical *pastorale.* Over and above the massive lists of their generally popular publications and the preparation of students, the collaboration of these centers led to significant invitational meetings held in such places as Ste. Odile, Montserrat, Munich, and Lugano. These study meetings made substantial proposals of liturgical reform, parallel to the interests of the liturgical commission of Pius XII, but going beyond the official commission's careful limits and expectations.[13]

The participants in these meetings formed the nucleus of specialists for later commissions: pre-conciliar or preparatory, conciliar and post-conciliar (the implementing Consilium set up in 1964 and the Congregation for Divine Worship, from 1969 to 1975). Their names should be listed in full, but a few familiar ones will suffice: Wagner, Jungmann, Fischer, Martimort, Gy, Roguet, Jounel, and many more. Of these the greatest was Josef Andreas Jungmann, who was both scholar and activist, and who received the rare and deserved honor of *Festschriften* on his sixtieth, seventieth, and eightieth birthdays. A mild and self-effacing priest, he was not unwilling to canvass the conciliar fathers and to enlighten and persuade them.

There is one general and public congress of the pre-conciliar period which needs to be specially mentioned, the Assisi-Rome meetings of 1956.[14] This congress evolved from the small study meetings already mentioned, but it was on a large and international scale and attended by an impressive group of bishops of the Church. For the first time both scholars and enthusiasts assembled in large numbers, including an invited delegation from North America, to consolidate in a public forum the progress of recent decades and to open the way to the (then unexpected) general council.

The official blessing on this gathering came first from the presidency of Cardinal Gaetano Cicognani, prefect of the Roman Congregation of Sacred Rites. Neither a liturgist nor a liturgiologist, the Cardinal was a benign and honorable proponent of liturgical renewal—chiefly noted later for his presidency of the Pontifical Preparatory Commission on the Sacred Liturgy (1960–1962). His death in early 1962 came when the schema of the Constitution was happily completed, but it created a serious gap in the months before the Council opened and indeed during the conciliar process itself.

The Assisi-Rome Congress placed before the whole church community the principal issues of liturgical restoration and reform, all the way from the vernacular question (still a matter of great sensitivity) and full lay participation in Christian worship to problems of cultural adaptation of the liturgy (in a notable address by Bishop van Bekkum of Indonesia).[15] The meeting was climaxed by an address in Rome by Pius XII, who confirmed the positions taken in the encyclical *Mediator Dei* of a decade earlier and cautiously opened the way to a future that would include, in his last days, a Roman instruction on music and the liturgy (September 3, 1958).

It is difficult enough to convey to a younger generation the vast difference between the Eucharist of today, even when indifferently or poorly celebrated, and the pre-conciliar style of stereotyped and passive service. Similarly, the pastoral and doctrinal climate of the 1950's in liturgical matters is hard to describe or recreate.[16]

The quality of the pre-conciliar enterprise was high, the insights great, the crystal ball clear enough, but the expectations were not so large as the event would justify. Above all, as has been stressed already, the educational and formational enterprise reached only a small number of parishes and parochial ministers.

The Influence of Other Movements

The fourth and final element in the liturgical picture of the 1940's and 1950's has already been hinted at. It is the strong parallel and relationship of the liturgical apostolate with other movements in the Church of that period. It is enough to mention these without much elaboration. Each had its place in the conciliar program, sometimes within, sometimes outside the *Constitution on the Sacred Liturgy.*

Just as the 1963 Constitution itself is biblically oriented, so was the liturgical movement deeply influenced by the developing *biblical scholarship* unleashed by Pope Pius XII. In candor, it must be said that there was not always a corresponding influence of liturgical promoters upon the biblical scholars, although in the United States common concerns met in such persons as John O'Connell of Chicago, Gerard Sloyan, and David Stanley.

Symbolic of the relationship with *the catechetical movement* was the academic background of Josef Jungmann himself, who was a catechetical pioneer even before he attained prominence as a liturgical scholar. His disciple, Josef Hofinger, combined catechetical and missiological concerns with liturgical renewal.

The *Constitution on the Sacred Liturgy* itself bears witness to the commonality of liturgical concerns with the revival of the arts at the service of public worship. Often, especially in the field of sacred or *liturgical music*, the marriage was a strident one, to which the Constitution bears ample witness. This is the explanation of the almost tiring insistence in Chapter VI of the Constitution on the active participation of the people in the sung liturgy, no matter how great the heritage of chant and polyphony to be preserved and fostered.

The 1950's saw, however, a flowering of genuine concern among architects—along with artists and artisans—for the liturgical function of church structures and embellishment, vesture and vessels, which would be suitable for celebration. Thus the openness of Chapter VII of the Constitution to all the *diverse forms of art* and its central concern for simplicity and suitability for celebration and congregational participation came as no surprise. In the United States, an earlier instance of this was the interest in a "liturgical brief" for architects and the Lercaro Awards for church architecture at Liturgical Weeks.

The *ecumenical movement* before the Council was a sleeping giant. It had little encouragement from Roman officialdom, but a receptive response in liturgical circles. One American instance was the Liturgical Week of 1960, which directly focused on the unity of the churches.[17] Examples could be multiplied from the pages of *Orate, Fratres*, whose subscription lists included many Christians of other communions. Again, the participation of observers from other Christian churches in the conciliar process—and later in the Consilium of liturgical implementation—had strong roots in the liturgical apostolate preceding the Council.

A final note could take us too far afield, but needs mention. The pages of *Orate, Fratres* perhaps best illustrate the relation of liturgical concerns to *the social, family, and lay movements* in the Church. This perspective, going back at least to Virgil Michel in the 1920's, was never lost sight of. It was greater in some liturgical promoters than others; and here, the names of Reinold Hillenbrand, H. A. Reinhold, Robert Hovda, and Thomas Carroll of Boston come to mind. Liturgical concerns were neither hothouse nor ivory tower. On the one hand, liturgical renewal and reform were not seen, at least in pre-conciliar days, as panaceas for social ills; on the other hand, an authentic liturgy was always understood as a commitment to what the Council would call "all the works of charity, piety, and the apostolate."[18]

The Conciliar Process

This is the context. The conciliar process itself, from 1959 to 1963 when the Constitution was issued, may be considered more briefly, again with some concentration on the American contribution, limited though this contribution may seem.

Possibly only historians and constitutional lawyers will be interested in the complexities of the parliamentary law or lack of parliamentary law in the Second Vatican Council. But the process, beginning in the winter of 1959 when Pope John announced his plan to call a council, is illustrative. And it did succeed in achieving an almost total consensus on liturgical matters among the Catholic episcopate assembled in the Holy Spirit for the four periods of the Council from 1962 to 1965.

On the eve of the Council's announcement, the Roman Congregation of Sacred Rites published its instruction on music and the liturgy (September 3, 1958), already mentioned. In the United States, the conference of bishops, which had balked at sponsoring the Liturgical Weeks when so requested by the

Benedictine abbots in the early 1940's, followed the lead of the French and German episcopates and set up the Bishops' Commission on the Liturgical Apostolate (now called the Bishops' Committee on the Liturgy) in 1958. In some measure it was designed to be a watchdog committee, but it had the advantage to be chaired initially by Cardinal Joseph Ritter of St. Louis and directed by Bishop James Griffiths of New York, who perhaps unexpectedly encouraged rather than discouraged the efforts of The Liturgical Conference. The Conference in its turn established a full-time office in Washington in the light of a decision taken at the 1959 meeting at the University of Notre Dame—a congress attended and graced by Cardinal Lercaro of Bologna.

The preparatory Commission on the Liturgy, named by Pope John in 1960, had as its task the review of the proposals for the Council submitted by the bishops, faculties and universities, and Roman departments.[19] It had as president Gaetano Cicognani, already mentioned, and as secretary Annibale Bugnini. Its members and consultors reflected scholarly and pastoral specializations; both groups included bishops and priests. Working by subcommittees, it produced a schema or draft in about fourteen months, under the guidance of Bugnini. The schema was notable for its breadth, for its reliance upon the experience of specialists, and for its faithful (and exceptional) attention to the proposals of the worldwide episcopate.

The hesitations with which the task was approached and the pressures from those unfriendly to liturgical reform are seen, for example, in the distribution throughout the final schema, and in the Constitution itself, of separate articles on the vernacular question. This matter was so sensitive that the subcommittee dealing with it was unable to submit a single, strong, and unified text. It hoped instead to move gradually to an acceptance of principle and specific application. As an instance of American involvement, one of the earliest versions of the critical text on regional and cultural adaptation of a revised Roman liturgy (articles 37–40 of the final document) was prepared by Johannes Quasten and Godfrey Diekmann in Washington, D.C.

The death of Cardinal Cicognani just before the commission's schema was ready to be submitted to the Central Preparatory Commission was a severe blow. The antipathy of his successor, Cardinal Arcadio Larraona, to both the schema and the secretary of the preparatory commission seemed to place the whole schema in some jeopardy. It received a mixed reception from the Central Preparatory Commission, but was little changed in the text transmitted to the conciliar fathers just before they assembled in the fall of 1962.[20] In fact, with all the apparent vicissitudes of the conciliar debate and the apparent setbacks in the course of emendation and re-emendation in 1962 and 1963, the final document emerged as simpler and stronger.[21]

Two and later three Americans participated in the conciliar commission, a body which was distinct from the earlier preparatory commission and was weakened by the loss of a number of specialists and especially of the competent secretarial role of Bugnini. The latter participated in the meetings of the conciliar commission, almost as a spectator, but was succeeded as secretary by Ferdinando Antonelli of the Congregation of Sacred Rites. Nonetheless the conciliar commission, with a majority of its members elected by the conciliar fathers, was a strong body. It listened carefully to the debate of the fathers during October and November 1962, and then set about the complex revision of the draft. Its task was complicated by the conflicting views expressed in the full debate and by continuing uncertainty whether an individual bishop spoke for himself alone or for a wide body of the fathers.

As in other debates during the Council, the bishops of the United States did not exercise a role in proportion to their large numbers. Some eighteen interventions on the liturgical schema are printed in Vincent Yzermans' excellent collection.[22] Cardinals Spellman and McIntyre, who took an almost entirely negative stance, gave the impression to the rest of the Council that the American Church was not prepared for liturgical change, partly because the very positive and open interventions of Cardinal Ritter of St. Louis were not immediately recognized as coming from an American. The equally as positive position taken by Archbishop Paul Hallinan of Atlanta, who had been elected to the conciliar commission on the liturgy, corrected this impression, as did thoughtful interventions by Bishop Victor Reed of Oklahoma City and Tulsa and others.

Archbishop Hallinan, a bishop for all seasons and for all good causes, deserves a slight digression, because he exemplified the sound and enthusiastic response of the conciliar fathers who came to the Council without strong liturgical presuppositions. A priest with major accomplishments in the Newman movement, and well prepared pastorally and academically, Hallinan served as *relator* for the conciliar commission in its report on Chapter III of the Constitution (about the sacraments other than the Eucharist). At the same time he was playing a major extra-conciliar role in the establishment of the International Committee on English in the Liturgy; this occurred in October 1963, by mandate of ten conferences of bishops in countries where English is spoken.[23]

Hallinan's chairmanship of the subcommittee on the sacraments illustrates the process. When the conciliar commission had digested the oral debate and the written interventions, it had to prepare a revised text and submit its proposals in the form of amendments for the vote of the general congregation or daily assembly of the Council. In the case of Chapter I of the Constitution, on the general principles of promotion and restoration, this had been accomplished in the first period of the Council (1962). In the case of Chapter III, it was Hallinan who in 1963 proposed and explained the amendments and variants in the text of Chapter III, after receiving the usual two-thirds majority approval from the whole commission for his report.

Next, when the amendments and the chapter as a whole had been voted upon, the commission had to consider the reservations or qualifications (the *modi*, some thousand in number for Chapter III) which the bishops had attached to their affirmative votes. Again it was Hallinan's role to respond to the questions raised and, in this instance, to propose a further amendment to extend the use of the vernacular to all parts of the sacramental rites. This time, with characteristic modesty, he delegated the formal presentation of the report to a colleague on the commission, the heroic Bishop Otto Spuelbeck of East Germany, an Oratorian long associated with the liturgical movement and a speaker at the 1956 Assisi-Rome congress.

This is only a suggestion of the process by which a consensus was reached on the entire *Constitution on the Sacred Liturgy*, each part being subjected to diligent scrutiny. During the initial debate in 1962 the ultimate fate of the schema was in great doubt—other schemata were effectively rejected by the Council—until a vote "in principle" was taken on November 14 of that year. There were only 46 negative votes out of 2,208, and from that moment it was clear that the conciliar fathers accepted the liturgical reform.

The complex process of amendment and reamendment of the liturgical schema went on, with about ninety distinct votes on specific matters, until the conciliar fathers ultimately voted to approve the final text on November 22, 1963, this time with only 19 negative notes out of 2,177. It remained for the Constitution to be approved and promulgated at a public session by Pope Paul VI and the other bishops on December 4—this time with four negative votes out of 2,151.[24]

The process says little about substance, with which the other following chapters of this collection are concerned. Unquestionably the *Constitution on the Sacred Liturgy* set the tone for the Council. To a degree it anticipated what was to be said in such documents as the Constitution on the Church and the Decree on the Pastoral Office of Bishops in the Church. In their deliberations the bishops had before them a draft prepared, as unhappily some other drafts were not prepared, first, with fidelity to the general purposes of Pope John in calling the Council and, second, with a careful reading of the recommendations from the entire Catholic episcopate that had been submitted during the so-called ante-preparatory period. Moreover, in judging the amendment process and the recommendations of the conciliar commission, the fathers had before them many of the explanatory notes called *declarationes* drawn up by the specialists of the preparatory commission.

If anything, some of the implementation of the Constitution, which was the work of the Consilium established in January 1964 by Pope Paul and headed by Lercaro with Bugnini as secretary, did not go so far as the conciliar fathers had reason to anticipate. The problems of the later period are illustrated by the successive versions of the *Ordo Missae* of 1967 and 1969.[25] These reflect a degree of retrogression and compromise.

The same point is illustrated by an observation dating from a still later period. In his fine commentary on the 1977 rite for the dedication of a church, Ignazio Calabuig describes the development of the revised rite after the setting up of a study group within the Congregation for Divine Worship in May 1970. The rite was approved in plenary session by the Congregation in May 1972. But he adds: "This project, subsequently reelaborated according to the particular outlooks and needs of other Roman departments, constitutes the immediate precedent for the rite . . ."[26] By 1977 the new Congregation for Divine Worship had been merged with the Congregation for the Sacraments, and Archbishop Bugnini had departed from the liturgical scene.

Such developments take us too far afield from the context and the process which culminated in the Constitution *Sacrosanctum Concilium* on December 4, 1963, four hundred years to the day since the Council of Trent entrusted the reform of the Roman liturgical books to the Roman See, an anniversary that has often been noted. Others will show how the document combines continuity with progress, restoration with accommodation, inner devotion with communal celebration, biblical and non-biblical sources, the *ecclesia* as mystery and the *ecclesia* as preeminently manifested in the liturgical assembly.[27]

This chapter has been an attempt to illustrate that the *Constitution on the Sacred Liturgy* did not appear suddenly or full blown, but grew out of a profound movement within the church community, a movement which believers would hold was a sign of the action of God's Spirit in the Church. Whatever the flaws, and they are not great, whatever the subsequent compromises, and again they are not great, the words of Burtchaell bear repeating: "The sacraments are in a tongue unloosed now, and can be celebrated with an imagination and an integrity that release more of their grace and power than before."

NOTES

1. See Carlo Braga, "Ricordo di Mons. Annibale Bugnini," *Notitiae* 193–194 (1982) 441–452, for a biographical note and tribute by a close collaborator of Bugnini's; also Gottardo Pasqualetti, "Una Vita per la Liturgia," in P. Jounel, R. Kaczynaski, G. Pasqualetti (eds.), *Liturgia: Opera Divina e Humana: Studi sulla riforma liturgica offerta a S.E. Mons. Annibale Bugnini in occasione del suo 70° compleanno* (Rome, 1982), pp. 13–28, for a lengthier essay, followed by a bibliography covering Bugnini's writings from 1939 to 1981 (pp. 29–41).

2. Letter to the editor of *The Washington Post*, July 1982.

3. See Thomas Richstatter, *Liturgical Law: New Style, New Spirit* (Chicago, 1977), pp. 181–208, for a select list of documents and chronicle of events from 1946 to 1975; R. Kevin Seasoltz, *New Liturgy, New Laws* (Collegeville, Minn., 1979), for a brief but thorough account of the liturgical development for the same period.

4. For example, Didier Bonneterre, *Le Mouvement Liturgique* (Escurolles, 1980).

5. James T. Burtchaell, "The Future of Our Fellowship," in *Commonweal*, Vol. 109, pp. 364–68, June 4, 1982.

6. November 20, 1947: *Acta Apostolicae Sedis* [=AAS] 39 (1947) 521–600. The Latin text is in Bugnini's valuable collection, *Documenta Pontificia ad Instaurationem Liturgicam Spectantia (1903–1953)* (Rome, 1953), pp. 96–164. English version in a similarly valuable collection, R. Kevin Seasoltz, *The New Liturgy, A Documentation, 1903 to 1965* (New York, 1966), pp. 107–159.

7. The *codex* was approved by John XXIII in an apostolic letter, *Rubricarum instructum* of June 25, 1960: *AAS* 52 (1960) 593–595. Commentaries: J. B. O'Connell, *The Rubrics of the Roman Breviary and Missal* (London, 1960); Frederick R. McManus, *Handbook for the New Rubrics* (Baltimore, 1961).

8. See the apostolic constitution of Paul VI *Missale Romanum* promulgating the reformed missal (April 3, 1969) and prefixed to that volume as well as the preface to the missal's General Instruction that was composed to rebut the "traditionalist" attack on the new Order of Mass. For a discussion of the canonical, theological, and liturgical misapprehensions of the critics, see Guy Oury, *La Messe de S. Pie V à Paul VI* (Solesmes, 1975).

9. The characterization was made by Pius XII on September 22, 1956, in an allocution to the Assisi-Rome International Congress on Pastoral Liturgy: *AAS* 48 (1956) 711–725; see *The Assisi Papers* (College-

ville, Minn., 1957), p. 224. Quoted without attribution in the Constitution on the Liturgy, no. 43.

10. The collection of *Proceedings* extends from 1940 to 1966, edited by a succession of elected secretaries of the Conference: W. Michael Ducey, O.S.B. (1940–1945), John P. O'Connell (1946), Shawn G. Sheehan (1947), Bede Scholz, O.S.B. (1948–1951), Aloysius G. Wilmes (1952-1957), William J. Leonard, S.J. (1958–1963), until the opening of a Washington secretariat of the Conference in 1960.

11. See Noel H. Barrett, *The Contribution of Martin B. Hellriegel to the American Catholic Liturgical Movement* (St. Louis, 1976); Frederick R. McManus, "Liturgical Pioneers and Parish Worship," in Mark Searle (ed.), *Parish: A Place for Worship* (Collegeville, Minn.), 1981, pp. 181–192.

12. Representative collections of writings by H. A. Reinhold, in addition to "Timely Tracts" in *Orate, Fratres,* are found in his *The American Parish and the Roman Liturgy* (New York, 1958); *The Dynamics of Liturgy* (New York, 1961).

13. For a resume of resolutions of some of these conferences, see H. A. Reinhold's own volume on the reform of the Roman Order of Mass: *Bringing the Mass to the People* (Baltimore, 1960).

14. Its proceedings are found in *The Assisi Papers,* a volume still worth reading and published as a supplement to *Worship,* 1957. The roster of speakers included such names as Jungmann, Capelle, Gerlier, Wagner, Bea, Roguet, van Bekkum, Rousseau, Garrone, Antonelli, Lercaro, Spuelbeck.

15. Wilhelm van Bekkum, "The Liturgical Renewal in the Service of the Missions," in *Assisi Papers,* pp. 95–112.

16. A current effort to recall—and perhaps to encapsulate through oral history and other means—the tone of the preconciliar liturgical apostolate is being made under the direction of William Leonard, himself a valiant pioneer of the American movement, at Boston College in June 1983. Appropriately this occurs at a university which has taken the lead in assembling liturgical and devotional materials from the period immediately preceding the Council.

17. *The Liturgy and Unity in Christ* (Washington, 1961).

18. Article 9.

19. These may be studied in the *Acta et Documenta Concilio Vaticano II Apparando, Series Prima*—for the antepreparatory period (from early 1959 to mid-1960).

20. *Acta et Documenta Concilio Vaticano II Apparando, Series Secunda,* covers the preparatory period, up to the opening of the Council itself,

although lacking the extensive documentation of the individual preparatory commissions.

21. The entire record of the general (daily) congregations and the (few) public sessions of the four periods of the Council (1962–1965) is contained in the magnificently edited and printed *Acta Synodalia*, unique in the history of general councils of the Church.

22. *American Participation in the Second Vatican Council* (New York, 1967).

23. See Frederick R. McManus, *ICEL: The First Years* (Washington, 1981).

24. For a summary account of the process and commentary, see Josef Jungmann, "Constitution on the Sacred Liturgy," in Herbert Vorgrimler (ed.), *Commentary on the Documents of Vatican II*, Vol. I (London and New York, 1967), pp. 1–87; Bonaventura Kloppenburg, "Chronicle of Amendments to the Constitution," in William Baraúna, *The Liturgy of Vatican II*, Vol. I (Chicago, 1966), pp. 71–94.

25. See Frederick R. McManus, "The Genius of the Roman Rite Revisited," *Worship* 54 (1980) 360–378.

26. *The Dedication of a Church and an Altar: A Theological Commentary* (Washington, 1980), p. 2.

27. A unique and indispensable collection of documents, conciliar and postconciliar, has recently been published in English; it is by far the most valuable documentary collection on the liturgical reform in any language: International Commission on English in the Liturgy, *Documents on the Liturgy 1963–1979: Conciliar, Papal, and Curial Texts* (Collegeville, Minn., 1982).

2
The Sacred Liturgy: Reform and Renewal

Edward Kilmartin, S.J.

On December 4, 1563, the fathers of the Council of Trent determined that the revision of the Roman Missal and the Divine Office be left to the Pope and his Curia. Four hundred years later to the date, the fathers of the Second Vatican Council approved the *Constitution on the Sacred Liturgy, Sacrosanctum Concilium.* Pope Paul VI promulgated it that same day. There are striking similarities which go beyond the historical dates, but also basic differences between the approaches of these two councils to the liturgy. A brief comparison may help.

The Council of Trent was a reform council aimed at removing heresies, renewing a *pastoral* episcopate and reforming morals. The Second Vatican Council had as its goal the renewal of the Church with the accent on progress. In the first period of the Council of Trent, the last two sessions took up the theology of sacraments. In the first period of the Second Vatican Council, the first item on the agenda was the draft of the *Constitution on the Sacred Liturgy.* The Council of Trent formulated statements about the theology of sacraments mainly directed at refuting erroneous or heretical teachings. The Second Vatican Council's teaching about the liturgy took another direction. It provided a theology, pastorally orientated, and intended to serve as the basis of the renewal and progress of the Church's liturgical life. The Council of Trent made a defense for time-honored liturgical practices and, at the same time, called for the removal of many abuses which had crept into the Mass. Vatican II acknowledged the relative poverty of the liturgical rites of the Roman liturgy and established norms and directives for the revision of all liturgical books. The Council of Trent was inspired by the vision of a unified Roman Mass and Breviary to be used by all local churches. Vatican II called for normative liturgical books and, at the same time, for adaptation to meet the needs of local churches. Trent left the matter of liturgical reform to the Holy See. Vatican II acknowledged the relative competence of "territorial bodies of bishops" in the work of adaptation of all liturgical rites.

The different approaches of the Council of Trent and the Second Vatican Council to the liturgy derive from the concrete historical contexts of both. Trent was preoccupied with the upheavals which threatened to dissolve the unity of the Church. Vatican II was concerned with modern cultural changes and their effects on the internal life of the Church. The fact that the liturgy took first place on the agenda of the Second Vatican Council was, at least partially, the result of the new awareness in theological circles of the importance of liturgy in the life of the Church. If one grants that the liturgy is the very heart of the life of the Church (SC 10), it follows that a reform council aimed at renewal of the life of the Church should begin with the renewal of liturgy.

The *Constitution on the Sacred Liturgy* provides an outstanding example of the attempt of Vatican II to respond to the challenge for a truly *pastoral* council, one which pays attention to all those factors which can make a substantial contribution to the renewal and progress of the Church. Its main importance lies in its theological description of the liturgy, which, in its pastoral orientation, stands in contrast to the abstract theological presentation found in the traditional theological manuals.

The Constitution's description of the liturgy offers a vision of the intrinsic unity of liturgy and sacraments; it brings to the foreground the role of all the participants as an expression of the Church at worship; it also offers practical norms and directives for modifying liturgical rites. These are intended to promote a more effective active participation of the whole worshipping community. However, it must be emphasized that this pastoral orientation derives from the theology contained in the Liturgy Constitution and is understandable only in the light of that theology.

Therefore, for us to reflect on the content of the *Constitution on the Sacred Liturgy*, to examine its pastoral orientation and to measure the success of its implementation, it is necessary for us to attempt at least partial answers to some foundational questions:

1. What are the main components of the theology of the liturgy in *Sacrosanctum Concilium?*

2. What is new about this theology?

3. What are some of the significant pastoral consequences which the Constitution draws from its theology?

4. How successful has the post-conciliar implementation of the theology and directives of the Constitution been?

5. What is the most basic presupposition for the success of the liturgical movement of our own day?

Theological Components

The *Constitution on the Sacred Liturgy* has made a substantial contribution to the theology of the liturgy by gathering together the proven findings of modern scholarship and producing a systematic presentation which elevated these findings from the consensus of theologians to a consensus of the teaching authority of the Church.

The heart of this theology is the work of redemption begun by God the Father and fully revealed and realized in the self-offering of Jesus—his death, resurrection and glorification. Jesus offered himself as man to the Father, not precisely to balance the scales of justice, i.e., to expiate for the sins of the world as a representative of sinful humanity in order to satisfy the demands of the just God. Rather, since salvation for human beings consists in the free acceptance of the loving self-communication of God, Jesus Christ, as head of all humanity, gave himself to the Father in complete openness in order to receive the full communication of the Father's personal love. His death becomes the manifestation of the victory of humanity over sin. Glorified by the Father in the Spirit, Jesus becomes Lord of history; he sends the Spirit from the Father to the world to be the abiding Source by which all humanity is drawn into union with him.

As the *Constitution on the Sacred Liturgy* teaches, the Paschal Mystery is, therefore, not only the cause of the salvation of the world but also the goal: the gathering of all into Christ, the Lord of history, and so into union with the Father in the Spirit. The Paschal Mystery is the origin, foundation and goal of the Church. This Holy People of God and Body of Christ participates now in the Paschal Mystery. It already shares, by way of anticipation, in the fulfillment of the Kingdom of God yet to come.

At the same time, this participation in the Paschal Mystery involves a task. The Church has the task of growing into the fullness of Christ by continually dying and rising with him and of drawing others into itself in the power of the Spirit so that God may be all in all. All the activity of the Church has the function of further revealing and realizing the work of redemption in partnership with Christ who is its active head. Thus, the Church's liturgy is a co-working of Christ and the Church—Christ always associating the Church with himself in the work of redemption. In the liturgy, sanctified in and through Christ, the holy people offers acceptable worship to the Father, is built up into a spiritual temple pleasing to God and so becomes an effective sign of salvation for the world.

Since the liturgy is the most expressive manifestation and realization of the work of redemption, it is the "summit and source" of all the Church's activity. All other activity of the Church is ordered to the liturgy and derives its orientation, inspiration and spiritual power from the liturgy. Consequently, the liturgy is not simply a means to an end; it has meaning in itself. It is not simply the place where Christians obtain spiritual nourishment for Christian action in the world; it is the activity in which the holy people of God is concretely manifested and realized, a real anticipation of the final gathering of all in Christ. Because the Eucharist expresses and realizes the Messianic Banquet of the Kingdom in the most profound way, it is the very summit of all ecclesiastical activity.

According to the Constitution, the liturgy contains in itself the meaning of all history; it displays the three dimensions of time—past, present and future—and their interrelationship. It recalls the Paschal Mystery in the most profound sense, as source of the community's subjective worship. Because of the personal presence of Christ, his historically past redemptive work is never past in its mystery. As foundation of the community's life it never ceases to be present in the liturgy as gift. Hence the here and now liturgy is a saving event. In it "the work of redemption is accomplished" (SC 2). The tangible liturgical celebration is both the action of God in Christ sanctifying the community and, at the same time, the grateful response of the believing community. As such the liturgy is a real participation in the final fulfillment. The Lord of the Church comes from the future, enters into the present liturgy and so effects a real anticipation of the eternal time when God will be all in all. In this holy time of the liturgy, past, present and future come together in an admirable synthesis. The deepest meaning of all reality is revealed and realized through Jesus Christ, "the same today as he was yesterday and as he will be forever" (Hebrews 13:8).

The Newness of This Liturgical Theology

The theology of the *Constitution on the Sacred Liturgy* is relatively new if one compares it to the post-Reformation Roman Catholic theology of liturgy.

1. The premise that liturgy is the most important activity of the Church is not new. But the explanation is new. Earlier Catholic theology based the importance of liturgical worship on

this argument: Worship of God is the highest activity of the personal creature. But the Church officially fulfills this exercise of the virtue of religion in its liturgy. Therefore liturgy is the highest activity of the Church from which it can expect divine blessings.

The Constitution, however, goes to the deepest level of the liturgical act. Does not the possibility of true worship of God originate from God's gift of the life of faith: the life in which we are so grasped by Christ that we become one with him and he with us? Does not true worship of God derive from Christ's present activity in the worshippers in the Spirit? The Constitution takes very seriously the theological significance of St. Paul's basic statements about worship, "The Spirit you received is not the spirit of slaves bringing fear into your lives again; it is the spirit of sons, and it makes us cry out, 'Abba, Father!' The Spirit himself and our spirit bear united witness that we are children of God" (Romans 8:15–16). "The proof that you are sons is that God has sent the Spirit of his Son into our hearts: the Spirit that cries, 'Abba, Father' " (Galatians 4:6).

In this perspective the Constitution describes the liturgy as a dialogue between God and the Community. It understands liturgy, first of all, as a divine action sanctifying the community and secondly as the response of believers. The double movement: God's sanctifying activity and the response of the community grounded in it, which takes place in and through the whole of the liturgical activity, constitutes the theological dimension of the liturgy and gives it its peculiar value.

2. The teaching of the Constitution that the liturgy is an activity of the whole Church is not new. But the explanation is new. Earlier theology understood the liturgy as the activity of those deputed officially to act in the name of the whole Church. The baptized laity were viewed as an audience linked vicariously through sympathetic participation in the experience of the ordained, who officially carried out the work of the Church. They were not considered direct subjects of the liturgical act!

Corresponding to this theology Pius XII states in the encyclical letter *Mediator Dei,* 1947, that the ordained alone are qualified "to perform those official acts of religion by which men are sanctified and God is duly glorified" (42). The Constitution's viewpoint clashes with this. For it makes the whole assembly the direct subject of the liturgical act: Liturgical services "are celebrations of the Church, namely, the whole people of God united and ordered around their bishops" (26.1).

3. The teaching of the Constitution about the intimate relationship between the liturgy as a whole and the seven sacraments of the Church also contains a new aspect. Earlier theology viewed the liturgy as the appropriate means of preparation for the reception of God's offer of grace in the sacraments. The Constitution overcomes the unreflective sharp distinction between liturgy as official exercise of the virtue of religion and the sacraments as means of salvation. The whole of the liturgy is understood to have the same basic structure: In the whole of the liturgical activity God in Christ is communicating sanctification and the community is responding in praise and thanksgiving.

In this connection the Constitution refers to the various modes of real presence of Christ in the whole of the liturgical action (SC 7.1), a teaching which goes beyond the narrow traditional emphasis on the presence of Christ in and through the Eucharistic species. Thereby the Constitution calls attention to the fact that all aspects of the liturgy have one purpose: to serve as a transparency for the active presence of Christ and so to draw the community into personal union with him and his Paschal Mystery and into worship of the Father.

Pastoral Consequences Drawn by the Constitution

The Constitution describes the liturgy as an act of communication between God the Father and his people in which Christ is the source of communication as mediator from the Father to the community and from the community to the Father. As chief speaker and actor of his Church, Christ continually communicates with the members of his Body. As a result they are made capable of interacting with their Lord and of offering worship to the Father.

From this perspective the Constitution concludes that all the participants of the liturgy have an active role to play and insists on the right and duty of all baptized to "full, conscious and active participation" (SC 14). Its norms and directives for realizing this goal are based on common sense. Conscious participation requires understanding of the meaning of the liturgy. Therefore the faithful must receive instruction and those responsible for this ministry must be given adequate training. Full and active participation is conditioned by a measure of simplification of rites and clarification of the link between what is said and done so that not much explanation will be required. Finally the Constitution calls for adaptation of normative rites to local conditions and cultural differences in the interest of fuller participation.

The Success of the Post-Conciliar Implementation

1. *Liturgical Formation*

The Constitution gave liturgical formation a high priority on the agenda of the renewal and progress of the liturgy. Post-conciliar Roman documents have been even more emphatic. In the matter of seminary training, the Constitution placed liturgy among the major courses and directed that instructors receive proper training in special institutes. Since then, the study of liturgy has been officially ranked immediately after biblical exegesis on the grounds that liturgy is the most important source of the living experience of faith and the tradition of faith. Numerous post-conciliar documents have also stressed (and in stronger tones than the Constitution) the active role of the laity in the liturgy. At the same time, they have repeatedly mentioned the serious responsibility of pastors to provide instruction for the laity inside and outside the liturgy.

However the proper implementation of the Constitution still awaits concrete action in many places. One often gets the impression that, in the training of seminarians, clergy and laity, Roman documents have not been read or are simply ignored.

2. *Simplification of Rites*

The Constitution called for simplification of rites so that they can be more easily understood. The heroic efforts of the post-conciliar commissions to honor this directive can only be applauded. However, one may ask whether the new rite of the Mass has actually attained the goal of the Council's directive, i.e., that it should not require much explanation. Is it too complicated to enable active participation? Is the Eucharistic Prayer, said aloud in the vernacular, really understandable to the average hearer with the range and depths of the concepts it expresses? Is it possible to state more clearly what the Eucharistic Prayer intends so that the participants will not have to read and ponder the text?

3. *Adaptation*

The Constitution recognizes that the worshipping community is both *speaker* and *hearer* of the Word of God. It also recognizes that human laws govern the possibility of communication in concrete local communities. Hence it favors the idea of local churches introducing, alongside official texts, other texts and viewpoints more appropriate to local cultural situations.

This conclusion is based not simply on the precedent that the one liturgy of the Church has been and is now expressed in various historically conditioned forms. More profoundly it is based on the fact that God speaks and acts in and through the various languages and cultures of the world.

To assure the unity of faith in an anticipated pluralism in liturgical forms within the Roman rite, the Constitution set down norms for hierarchical regulation. These norms are new in that they acknowledge and favor the relative transfer of competence in liturgical matters to "competent territorial bishops," while at the same time recognizing the final responsibility of the Apostolic See (SC 22).

The principle of subsidiarity in matters of the government

of liturgical practice by bishops is based on the theology of the episcopate. Since the Church has an episcopal structure, the bishops, as leaders of dioceses, have the responsibility for the fostering of the spiritual life of the members. This principle also corresponds to the Second Vatican Council's understanding of the Church as a communion: a unity concretely realized by dialogue between Rome and the hierarchy of local churches and between the local hierarchy and members of the diocese. This principle also corresponds to common sense. Centralistic regulations almost inevitably involve final decisions by authorities who have little or no acquaintance with the various geographical areas and their mentalities. Such general regulations tend to suppress the freedom of expression in local churches which enables a more authentic celebration of the faith.

But the deepest theological grounds for the principle of subsidiarity must be found in the fact that the Spirit is at work in the local churches and in the cultures of the local churches. The Spirit leads local churches to formulate the optimum expression of the liturgical memorial of the Paschal Mystery in their own languages and cultures. In the Spirit, it may be taken for granted that the local churches can best determine that they need to foster the renewal of worship and that this will necessarily involve the use of cultural means which link the participants together.

The post-conciliar dialogue between Rome and territorial bishops in the matter of adaptation has only partially succeeded. The results of an unmistakable tendency toward increasingly centralistic administration in liturgical affairs, however, do not cast doubt on the general principle supported by the *Constitution on the Sacred Liturgy:* The renewal and progress of the Church, in all areas of life including the liturgy, can only take place in a dialogue between the Church and various cultures and, in this context, between all the local churches of the One, Holy, Catholic and Apostolic Church.

4. *Special Age Groups in the Church*

The Constitution called for a special rite of Infant Baptism and so acknowledged this special age group in the Church. As a consequence, Rome provided the 1973 *Directory for Masses with Children.* The opening paragraph gives the reason: "The Church is bound to be specially concerned about the welfare of children who . . . have not received Confirmation . . ."(1).

The observation prompts anyone who has been engaged in pastoral ministry to ask: What about the youth group? Human sciences take youth seriously and so should the Church. It is extremely important that they be able to express their lives, their hopes and aspirations in the liturgy. Indeed, as baptized they have the right and duty to full, conscious and active participation.

The youth subculture has its own rituals, foreign to the Roman rite, but not to more archaic forms of worship: the play of lights, music as expression of life, dance. Obviously, forms of youth culture should not be simply added to the liturgy. The lack of proper integration can and does lead to an active participation at odds with the spirit of the liturgy. But the effort should be made to explore what forms of youth culture can qualify for liturgy. One might hope that a special youth Mass could be created not to separate this group from the rest of the adult community, but to enable it to experience the depth of the liturgy in a way which would carry over to the more adult celebration.

5. *Other Problems Concerning Active Participation*

There are many other concrete problems concerning active participation of the laity in the liturgy. Only some of them can be mentioned here. The Constitution ranks the homily as "part of the liturgical service" and so recognizes that the personal witness of faith is a constitutive part of the liturgy. It assumes that the ordained will always give the homily at Mass. The *Third Instruction on the Implementation of the Constitution,* 1970, states that the priest preaches the homily and the laity should refrain from comments and dialogue (2a). The only exception to the rule is given in *The Directory for Masses with Children.* Here it is said that a lay person may preach if the priest has difficulty adapting himself to the mentality of children.

However from a theological point of view the priest is also hearer of the Word. Why may not a qualified lay person, on the basis that all charisms are intended for the common good, be allowed at times to preach at an adult Mass? Moreover on suitable occasions in smaller groups, there seems to be no theological reason why the priest could not invite a personal witness of faith, as part of the liturgical service, from the other active participants. Indeed, in this way, the dependence of all on Christ, both priest and laity, could be effectively manifested.

The theme of active participation of all in the liturgy raises the question about the traditional role of women. As yet we have no favorable decisions about the appointment of women as acolytes or lectors, to say nothing of ordination to offices which involve liturgical leadership, such as the diaconate. There still exists in the Orthodox Jewish Prayer Book the blessing of Yahweh in which men thank God for not making them women. This prayer clearly supposes that women are not the direct subject of the worship of God. No such prayer exists in official Roman Catholic liturgy. The "we" of the liturgy includes both women and men. But the practical consequences of this are still to be worked out.

One last serious problem on the right and duty of all baptized to actively participate in the liturgy deserves mention. The Constitution views the Eucharist as constitutive of the Church. Without the regular celebration of the Eucharist, therefore, a community can hardly be expected to survive for a long time as a truly Christian community. From this, one can conclude that all Christian communities have the right to an ordained leader who can preside at the Eucharist because of their right, as baptized, to the celebration of the Eucharist. Therefore in the present situation of a lack of a sufficient number of ordained priests, the question can be asked: Should the right of a community to the Eucharist, and so to a priest, remain unfulfilled because in some particular local churches there cannot be found candidates asking for ordination who have enough training in formal theology to be called theologians and, at the same time, are celibates?

A Basic Presupposition for the Success of the Liturgical Renewal

A few months after the promulgation of the *Constitution on the Sacred Liturgy*, Romano Guardini sent a message to a liturgical conference in Mainz, Germany. For about half a century his writings had inspired great love and understanding of the liturgy. But his word to the conference came in the form of this question: Is the modern Christian capable of the liturgical act?

Behind this question lies the further question: If, in our day to day living and the reality around us, animate and inanimate nature, social contacts, etc. are valued insofar as they are useful for our individual human needs, what will be our understanding of liturgy? In fact autonomous human reason has established through its practice concrete dimensions of reality and their basic structures. It has created "necessities of life" which seem altogether necessary for the good life. It has made humanity, created to be loving and giving, into a consumer society which measures success by material possessions. This consumer culture leads people to identify themselves with what they have and they are so judged by others. This society has even profaned the nature of play! The game is not the thing, the winning is all.

In this context it is extremely difficult for a person to recognize self as an inviolable person of absolute value and so approach the others in the same way. It is difficult for an individual to be convinced that he or she grows through relating to a personal God and to other personal human beings in a deeply loving and personal way, one which accepts the other as other and gives thanks for the other's otherness.

The liturgy offers another experience of reality. Through its texts and rites it uncovers the meaning of all created reality around us: that it is a gift of the loving God intended to draw personal beings into a response of love of God and so into union with the one who is God of all. Thus it is calculated to awaken the experience that all personal beings are daughters and sons of the one God and prompts the believer to serve as instrument of God's loving entrance into the world of other human beings by their love of neighbor. In this way liturgy can serve as source of ethical conduct for Christians in daily life.

But this liturgical view of the meaning of human existence is only plausible and credible to the extent that it actually becomes the orientating center and source of power for all activity of Christians in all spheres of life. In other words, the liturgy can contribute to the renewal and progress of the Church only if it derives from the stability of an adult community which witnesses through the liturgy that its stability is owed, founded on the Paschal Mystery of Jesus Christ. Only so will a deeper structure of the world be really experienced and publicly placed over against that produced by modern science.

For this to happen requires a living faith in the one who is the chief actor and speaker of the liturgy, Jesus Christ. In the time of the *profanation* of the world we have an important word which comes to us from the past. In 1 Peter 1:16, we are told: "Become holy yourselves in every aspect of your conduct, after the example of the Holy One who called you . . . Be holy, for I am holy."

Jesus himself is quoted in John 17:19 as saying: "I consecrate myself." This consecration of himself and all humanity, which he represents, as well as the whole world, which he as Word created, is the range of the Christian liturgy. It is, in short, the spirit of the liturgy—that vocation to which all Christians are called. If Christians do not understand this, they no longer know what the ancient heathens knew: that all things, the home, the table, the fields and woods, time itself, possess a deeper meaning than is understood by our age of enlightenment.

Christian liturgy will only succeed and become the "summit and source" of all the Church's activity, to the extent that the participants come to know and accept the meaning and demands made by the words of the Roman Canon: "We offer to you, God of glory and majesty, this holy and perfect sacrifice . . ." As long as a Christian community does not know what the sacrifice of the Holy One, the Christ, demands of it, its liturgy is a failure. On this subject the words of Cardinal Josef Ratzinger, written at the conclusion of Vatican II, may serve as a closing challenge for all of us:

> For the Church, worship is a matter of life and death. If it no longer succeeds in drawing the faithful to worship, and indeed so that they accomplish worship, then it has lost its title to existence.

3
The Sacred Liturgy: Development and Directions

R. Kevin Seasoltz, O.S.B.

Commenting on the ecclesial reform set in motion by the Second Vatican Council, Yves Congar pointed out that it "was a reform made from above—a fairly unusual phenomenon—which was not prepared for from below."[1] In setting out to reform the liturgy, the Council moved to change one of the more sensitive areas in Catholic life, for in many ways the liturgy is the stage on which Catholic identity is acted out.[2] There were many people, both priests and laity, who welcomed the image that was projected by the reformed liturgy; some of them had kept in touch with the modern liturgical movement and had been formed so as to root their spirituality primarily in the Church's liturgy rather than in secondary devotions. But there were many others whose Catholic identity was in fact rooted in memories, feelings, and ritual patterns which were abruptly dislodged and sometimes destroyed by reforms in the liturgy and other aspects of Church practice and belief. There is no doubt that rigid structures, inflexible liturgies and devotions, and unquestioned doctrinal statements did give the impression that the Catholic Church never changed, thus assuring its members a sense of stability and security. But hindsight is often excessively optimistic. From an aesthetic and pastoral point of view, the pre-conciliar worship certainly left much to be desired. As Archbishop Rembert Weakland noted recently, very little music of any value was sung in the average American parish before the Second Vatican Council; "the general fare was indeed in bad taste."[3]

The reaction to the conciliar reforms on the part of many people was indeed quite painful, for as Congar noted, the institutional Church imposed changes from above, without adequate preparation of those most immediately affected by the changes. Among pastors there was a sense of loyalty and goodwill and a conviction that one should do what the Church required, but that loyalty and goodwill were put under severe pressure in the years following the Council. What was missing above all among priests, religious and educators was a grasp of the theological principles underlying the reforms and a sense of the historical processes which led up to them. Above all Catholics found it difficult to sense continuity between the new and the old. As the momentum of reform accelerated in the late 1960's and early 1970's, many people experienced not only confusion but also deep anger.

It is hard to know how the pain could have been avoided; reform had to start somewhere. The fact is that the whole process of liturgical reform was fraught with anxiety and polarization, from which the Church still suffers.[4] The confusion has been magnified by extensive cultural developments throughout the world; conflicts in the Church have often paralleled and reflected conflicts in the secular world. Likewise the growth of cultural pluralism in the world had stimulated the growth of cultural pluralism in the Church, a growth that has manifested itself on theological, liturgical, and structural levels. Both the secular and ecclesial scenes are marked by crisis, complexity and an urgent quest for solutions to urgent problems. That both the world and the Church are in a state of crisis is evident enough, but an analysis of the situation is extremely difficult because of the multiplicity of factors involved, many of which seem to be mutually contradictory. An informed awareness of these factors is essential, however, for any on-going renewal of the Church and its liturgy. Otherwise we are in grave danger of continuing to update both the Church and the liturgy on the basis of a narrow or superficial understanding of what the signs of the times and contemporary Catholics really need.[5]

In the past two decades the Holy See has issued numerous liturgical decrees and instructions as well as promulgated revised rites for various liturgical celebrations. These documents have been interpreted in a variety of ways, some of which have been at odds with each other. At times the texts have been situated in their appropriate context and efforts have been made to probe and grasp the historical and theological background of what has been stated in the documents so that proper pastoral, liturgical, and aesthetic judgments might be made in implementing directives. Such efforts have usually resulted in a sound revitalization of the Church's liturgical life. At other times, the texts have been looked upon as sterile statements of theory or practice, subject to no ambiguity and hence allowing no measure of nuanced interpretation. In such instances the liturgical practice of the Church has simply meant a continuation of that rubrical mentality which prevailed in most areas of the Roman Catholic Church from the sixteenth century down to our own time.[6] In other instances, the legalism which prevailed before the Council gave way to a new antinomianism whereby irresponsible ministers proceeded "to change anything and everything in the name of progress and 'pastoral need'."[7]

On April 3, 1980, the Sacred Congregation for the Sacraments and Divine Worship issued the instruction *Inaestimabile donum* on certain norms concerning the worship of the Eucharist.[8] It noted in passing and with approval various positive aspects of the liturgical reform, including deeper involvement of the laity in the Christian mysteries, doctrinal and catechetical enrichment brought about by greater exposure to the Bible and by the use of vernacular languages, the development of a sense of community in Christian worship, and a better understanding of the relationship between liturgy and life. But the bulk of the document was devoted to a denunciation of what it termed "frequent abuses being reported from different parts of the world."[9] If there are abuses (and there are), they should certainly be corrected. However, the instruction from the Holy See should also have addressed itself to the frequent abuse of authority and the failure to minister responsibly on the part of those who have either consistently opposed or given mere lip service to liturgical renewal.

Furthermore, there is the simple fact that the Sacred Congregation for the Sacraments and Divine Worship has not encouraged liturgical indigenization and cultural adaptation of the new rites, and so it has failed to implement the final stage of liturgical reform called for by the Second Vatican Council itself. On an official level the impression has been given that the primary goal of the *Constitution on the Sacred Liturgy* has been simply the restoration of purified ancient rites. Certainly such restoration has been useful, but the Constitution itself has shown in its opening paragraphs that liturgical renewal must go beyond the simple stage of restoration: "It is the goal of this most sacred Council to intensify the daily growth of Catholics in Christian living; to make more responsive to the requirements of our times those Church observances which are open to adaptation; and to strengthen those aspects of the Church which can help summon all of humanity into her embrace. . . . The Council also desires that, where necessary, the rites be carefully and thoroughly revised in the light of sound tradition, and that they be given new vigor to meet the circumstances and needs of modern times."[10]

In general, the *Constitution on the Sacred Liturgy* took a profoundly theological and pastoral approach to the celebration of Christian faith, an approach which stands in marked contrast to the rigid attitude we formerly assumed in liturgical matters. The conciliar decision to cast the document in the form of a constitution rather than a decree or declaration implied a decision to join disciplinary or practical measures with theoretical or theological exposition. This decision established a format for setting out subsequent liturgical documents, especially the revised rites themselves which usually combine in the *praenotanda* the theological underpinnings for the rite and the directives for executing the rite. In setting out the theological foundations as well as practical directives the Council above all attempted to help people think of liturgical matters differently as well as execute rituals differently. Experience, however, has shown that it is easier to do things differently than it is to think of them in different terms. Certainly it was the Council's intention that reform in liturgical theology and practice should go hand in hand so that people would in fact understand the reforms and the reforms themselves would deepen the spiritual life of the people.[11] Implementation of the Council's approach of course depends on both expertise and excellence in liturgical leadership, planning, and celebration; it can only be hampered by untrained amateurs whose haphazard and inept efforts usually distort the celebration of the Christian mysteries and inhibit the development of Christian faith.

One of the major failures in the Church's efforts at liturgical renewal has undoubtedly been the failure of leadership. As Mark Searle has noted, this is said without the intention of assigning blame to anyone in particular, for bishops and priests, as well as the Roman Curia itself, are just as much product of their own histories as anyone else.[12] It must simply be acknowledged that at every level of the Church's life there has been a significant lack of conviction about the centrality of the liturgy in the Christian economy. Nevertheless there are many people today who are doggedly looking for spiritual strength and support in a liturgical context but they search in vain. Convinced that the Church is the right way to salvation, they are frustrated by their actual experiences of the Church as they are exposed to Catholic preaching which often lacks spiritual depth and conviction and which is out of touch with their day-to-day struggles. Instead of being nourished by liturgical rituals which are vital, they find the fare that is offered both bland and anemic. As various surveys have shown, most priests in this country are simply unprepared to perform effectively the liturgical roles set out in the revised orders for celebration. Recent studies have noted that seminarians and young priests are no better off than older priests in the ministry, for liturgical studies are often approached haphazardly in seminaries with the result that newly ordained ministers are ill-prepared to lead people effectively in prayer and celebration.[13]

It has been suggested that at the root of the problem concerning liturgical leadership is the issue of power.[14] That hypothesis would help to explain the Roman Curia's reluctance to allow national hierarchies to be responsible for the liturgical life of their churches; it would help us understand why local bishops are reluctant to exercise initiative and creativity and to allow others to do so; it would give us some insight into why most priests feel insecure and weary as they find themselves badgered on the right by those who want fewer reforms, on the left by those who want more reforms, and by those above who want their directives implemented promptly and effectively. Most church leaders, even younger ones, have been trained in a predominantly institutionalized model of the Church where some men are in control and other men and all women are controlled. One is reminded of the paranoid complaint of Pope Alexander VII in the seventeenth century: "We have learned with great sorrow that in the kingdom of France certain sons of perdition, itching with novelties detrimental to souls, and despising the laws and practice of the Church, have lately come to such madness as to dare to translate the Roman Missal and to hand it over to persons of every rank and sex."[15] There is no doubt that in the past two decades lay people have developed a sense of ownership in liturgical matters. They identify with the Council's assertion that "liturgical services are not private functions, but rather celebrations of the whole Church."[16] They see themselves as the Church. Understandably many of them are disillusioned or angered when their church leaders fail them or when they see liturgical reforms grounded because of clerical authoritarianism.

Shift from Classicist to Empiricist Notion of Culture

Underlying and contributing to much of the tension in the Church during the past twenty years has been a shift from a classicist to an empiricist notion of culture. An understanding of the nature of this shift is important because it has significant implications on the liturgical level and helps to explain why people respond so differently to liturgical reforms and why such diverse interpretations are often given to liturgical documents. For centuries Roman Catholics generally espoused a classicist view of culture. Culture has been defined in various ways, but for our purposes Bernard Lonergan's definition of culture as a "set of meanings and values informing a common way of life" is useful.[17] A classicist view of culture maintains that there is but one culture which is normative, universal and permanent. The values it embraces and the meanings it communicates are universal in claim and scope. It appeals to an abstract ideal and its concerns are unchanging; it attends to universals rather than particulars. It is informed by so-called classical philosophy, structured according to Aristotelian logic, and issues laws which are universally applicable and truths which are eternal. Circumstances of time and place are accidental in a classical matrix. Humanity itself is a universal concept reflecting an unchanging reality.[18]

When a classicist understanding of culture prevails, theology is looked upon as a permanent achievement; theologians simply discourse on its given nature. Liturgy is concerned with the uniform worship of God; as such it reflects the unchanging nature of both God and his people and the constant relationships that should prevail among them. As the cultural expression of the life of the Church, liturgy also enshrines a particular understanding of the Church as a perfect hierarchically structured society. It is wedded above all to an institutional model of the Church and is most comfortable with a descending christology. Ideally its permanence and uniformity are symbolized by a common unchanging language, such as Latin, and its execution is directed by well-defined, universally applicable rubrics. If the classicist speaks of cultural adaptation or liturgical indigenization, it is simply a matter of incidentals undergoing minor adjustments.[19]

The liturgical rites which were promulgated following the Council of Trent were singularly uncontextualized; in fact people generally never imagined that the liturgy celebrated according to those rites should in any way be affected by the diverse and wide-ranging social, economic, political and educational situations prevailing throughout the Church of the Roman Rite. The books made possible the uniform worship of God throughout the Western Catholic world; they reflected what was considered true religion as opposed to Protestantism in particular and all non-Catholic religions in general which were looked upon as simply heretical; and they promoted a sense of stability and security over against the transitoriness and relativism of the secular world.[20]

Unfortunately classicist culture has failed to realize an important factor which relativizes its normative value for people today. It has not been sufficiently aware of its own historical conditioning, as well as the historical self-making of individual persons and social groups, including those deeply committed to a classicist world-view. As more and more Roman Catholics become aware of its limitations, they are rejecting a classicist notion in favor of an empiricist notion. The contemporary empiricist approach to culture acknowledges that there are as many cultures as there are distinct sets of values and meanings.[21] Articulated in a variety of philosophies, sociologies, anthropologies, and social psychologies, contemporary empiricist culture recognizes the historical and relative character of the means by which it communicates meanings and values. It attempts to understand principles not in the abstract but as they operate in changing contexts. It is concerned primarily with the particular rather than the universal, and it sees each human institution as the product of a specific history of efforts to satisfy human needs and wants and to sustain what is deemed worthwhile.[22]

When an empiricist notion of culture prevails, theology is conceived as an on-going process to be carried out in the context of modern science, philosophy, history, and scholarship in general. The Church itself is looked upon as a structured process; it is an out-going process, existing not simply for itself but for all of humanity. Ecclesiology is apt then to be expressed not so much in terms of an institutional model but in terms of a community of disciples seeking to respond to the on-going gift of God's revelation of himself in Jesus Christ. Such an ecclesiology is usually supported by an ascending christology which sets out the life, death and resurrection of Christ as the model for humanity in its efforts to reach out to the divine initiative offering salvation to all. The goal in all of this is the reign of

God not only within the Church's own organization but in all societies, not only in life hereafter but in life here and now. If the constitutive meaning and values of Christianity are to be shared with all the people of this world, Church teachers and preachers must not only broaden their horizons to include an accurate and intimate understanding of the diverse cultures they address, but they must also grasp the innate resources of those cultures and utilize them creatively so that, in Lonergan's words, "the Christian message becomes, not disruptive of the culture, not an alien patch superimposed upon it, but a line of development within the culture."[23] If the liturgy is one of the principal cultural expressions of the life of the Church and also one of its primary means of evangelization, what is true of the Church is especially true of the liturgy, which is, as the *Constitution on the Sacred Liturgy* affirms, "the summit toward which the activity of the Church is directed" and "the fount from which all her power flows."[24]

Although the post-Tridentine liturgical books, so tightly controlled and so uniformly implemented, gave the impression of being a-cultural, historical studies have shown that they were indeed highly conditioned culturally and reflected the social, political, and theological contexts in which they were originally compiled. It has become clear that liturgies have regularly been carriers of political and social meanings and power.[25] In the centuries following the promulgation of the post-Tridentine liturgical books, Roman Catholic adaptation of worship forms to culture took place almost exclusively in the area of religious devotions, a phenomenon peculiar to the Roman Church. This often resulted in the alienation of the community or at least the distancing of the community from the officially approved liturgy, especially as the community's culture became more and more diversified. It also meant that the community's religious life was sustained and fostered primarily by extra-liturgical experiences.[26]

Since the Second Vatican Council, Christianity in general has been undergoing a cultural transition of magnitude unknown since Paul brought the Gospel to the Greeks. This has meant that the actual makeup of the human consciousness of many Christians has undergone transformation and that the way they conceive and express their religious beliefs has changed. Contemporary liturgical reforms in the Catholic Church have to some extent at least been carried out so as to respect and reflect what has been happening in the lives of modern people.

However, the response to the undeniable prevalence of cultural pluralism in the Roman Church today is mixed. There is often uneasiness on the part of the Roman Curia and many bishops lest they lose control of the community when such diversity exists. Pluralism is sometimes looked upon as inherently heterodox.[27] Then there are those who are nostalgic for the unity and security which classicist culture brought to many people. Curiously, some of these people openly acknowledge the legitimacy of an empiricist culture in all areas of their lives except religion, where they expect life to go on unchanged. They can live with twentieth-century physics, sociology, economics, and technology, but they want sixteenth or seventeenth-century religion. Their Church should be *semper idem.* This of course results in an absolute disjunction between religion and life. Others identify culture with artistic forms. Disgruntled by what they see as a trendy pursuit of cultural fads in the areas of music and art and nostalgic for the aesthetic experiences they had or imagined they had in the pre-conciliar days, they oppose any adaptation of liturgy to culture and insist that culture must adapt itself to what they think should be an unchanging liturgy.[28] Others reject the empiricist approach to culture altogether and remain convinced that the classicist culture, based as it is on a *philosophia perennis,* is the only legitimate culture and should be defended and preserved at all costs.

The complex situation created by this plurality of world-views, some of which are diametrically opposed to one another, results in much unresolved conflict in the Roman Church today. The liturgy above all is the target of much hostility, and the liturgical assembly is often the context in which the conflict is acted out. Because of a diversity of world-views it is quite possible that within a particular liturgical assembly one group of people will find the celebration deeply expressive and constitutive of their faith while the others will find the experience alienating and demoralizing. There is a great need for education concerning the whole matter of culture, so that people are able to name and appropriate the cultural matrix out of which they operate. They must be able to understand the nature of the differences that divide them, and hopefully come to the conclusion that liturgy should always take on characteristically plural forms, given the historically diverse cultures in which it finds itself.[29]

Developments in Hermeneutics

The shift from a classicist to an empiricist understanding of culture has affected and promoted developments in another area which has significant implications for liturgy and the interpretation of liturgical texts. It is the area of hermeneutics. A complicated but extremely important discipline, hermeneutics is concerned with the interpretation of texts which are treated primarily as works rather than objects. The distinction between "object" and "work" is basic to contemporary hermeneutical discussions.[30] An object is part of the natural world, such as a tree, a table, or a rock, whereas a work is a human expression or achievement. Looked at from different points of view, texts are of course both objects and works; however it is above all as human works that texts are subjected to interpretation. They are looked at not primarily as objects to be analyzed but as human expressions and achievements which mediate meaning.[31]

In order to achieve its goal, hermeneutics first of all relies on sound exegesis. To accomplish exegesis at the highest professional level, one must have knowledge of the languages in which the texts were originally written; one must be capable of using the tools of textual criticism; and one must have sufficient historical background, including a comprehensive knowledge of the development of the texts and a familiarity with the history of the interpretations that have previously been given to the texts.[32]

However, the primary purpose in studying the texts is not to decompose them into their constitutive parts in order to account for their origins but rather to grasp the meaning of the texts in their integrity, including the personal context out of which they have emerged and the context in which they are appropriated by others. The goal of hermeneutics is not to set out empirically verifiable statements about texts but to facilitate the dialogical illumination of the meaning of the text and the self-understanding of the one appropriating the text through reading or hearing. The meaning of the text with which hermeneutics is preoccupied is really the synthesis which results from a dialogue between the world of the interpreter and the world of the text. As Paul Ricoeur notes, the sense of the text is not behind it but in front of it; it is not something hidden in the past when the text was composed but something disclosed in the possible world which the text projects for the reader or hearer.[33] The meaning of a text, then, is not limited to what the author originally intended, even though it was originally produced to express such an intention. In being exteriorized in writing, a text is given an independent existence, open to anyone who can read or hear and it means then whatever it means when it is taken into the world of the one who receives it.

Because a text is a linguistic work rather than an object, it is polysemous; in other words, it is open to various interpretations. Due to the polyvalence of words, the meaning of a linguistic work cannot be reduced to one, univocal, empirically verifiable sense; the work will generate various interpretations in different readers or hearers because they bring different worlds of meaning to the task of interpretation.[34]

Before the contemporary developments in hermeneutics, it was generally presumed that the historical distance between the originator of a text and the interpreter was a disadvantage to accurate understanding of the meaning, but now that distance is not looked at as an obstacle but as an advantage, provided the world of the interpreter has in fact been enriched by the intervening tradition, thus facilitating the appropriation of more meaning than was available to those who lived at the time the text was originally composed. In other words, subsequent interpreters might well operate within much wider horizons than those of a former period.[35] This is not necessarily so, however;

just as one's horizon may enlarge throughout life, so also it may diminish. A later age may in fact experience and interpret life in a narrower context than those which preceded it. For that reason, it is important that one grasp the relationship between the sense and the reference of a text. The sense is internal to the sentences that make up a text; it is constituted by the relation between subject and predicate. A sentence such as "religious profession is one of the seven sacraments" makes sense, but the reference, i.e. the relation of the sense to reality, is falsified because religious profession is in fact not one of the seven sacraments.[36]

In the interpretation of texts, the primary concern is with the meaning of the text itself rather than with the author's meaning. This is the principal difference between contemporary hermeneutics and traditional exegesis or historical criticism. The latter is concerned with reconstructing the author's meaning by deciphering the sense of the text in its proper historical context. In contrast, contemporary hermeneutics is concerned with understanding the meaning of the text in terms of its reference and truth claims now. The meaning will be valid and true to the extent that the world of the text is accurately set out and brought into dialogue with the world of the interpreter.

It is important to note that literary texts are symbolic; they are not simple signs setting out information or exposing data. They reveal reality that goes beyond the limits of the texts themselves. They invite us to come to terms with their meaning and challenge us to inhabit their world. Because they supply a limited amount of explicit information, they require us to fill in the blanks. Consequently exposure to symbolic texts is naturally apt to result in diverse interpretations and experience on the part of various participants. Since they demand participation rather than inspire mere recognition by detached observers, texts are power-laden.[37] In a sense, then, texts are open-ended. By engaging in them, by inhabiting their world, people discover new meanings, new values, new motivations, and new horizons for their lives. Because they are open-ended, texts can expand, grow, and deepen; likewise our experience of texts can change—it can expand or contract. To think of texts, then, as changeless reminders of bald facts or simple truths is to convert texts as symbols into mere signs. Texts are pliant, flexible, and supple. Their relation to people is reciprocal in the sense that they disclose new potentials for human life, but they also are shaped and refined or even distorted by the changing circumstances of life.[38]

Hermeneutics and Liturgical Texts

In the years before the Second Vatican Council, liturgical texts, as well as canonical texts in general, were looked upon not as polyvalent but as univalent. Within a classicist culture, they were evaluated in terms of their precision, the clarity of their meaning, and the absence of ambiguity. The ideal was to formulate texts in a way that left no room for doubt in the mind of the reader. There were of course traditional canonical principles such as epikeia, intrinsic cessation of law, and excusing causes which provided some measure of relief for those who found norms in conflict with pastoral goals.

But conciliar and post-conciliar liturgical law has taken on a distinctive style and its own characteristic features. Unlike the rubrics found in the pre-conciliar liturgical books, it is flexible and adaptable, it is generally interested in the totality of the liturgy and the integrative relationships among its parts, it is reflective of the doctrinal foundations of the liturgy, and it is intent on promoting the pastoral and spiritual goals of the liturgy. In the years following the Council, a number of canonists took the old canonical categories of epikeia, excusing causes, and intrinsic cessation of law and applied them to the new liturgical documents;[39] the results, however, were not very satisfactory. Writing in *The Jurist* in 1968, Walter Kelly frankly labelled concepts such as epikeia and intrinsic cessation as "outmoded weapons" used against a "moribund opponent for an indefensible position." He acknowledged the need for some "new ground," and some "virgin territory" for interpreting the new liturgical texts.[40]

Some authors have approached the problem in terms of authority and obedience; they point out that the new style and spirit of the post-conciliar liturgical law demand a new style of obedience.[41] That approach, however, is simplistic because it overlooks the more basic concern, namely, that of interpretation or hermeneutics. Obedience is a later response which follows previous discernment and understanding of some value. Sound interpretation is obviously a complex task, but when we do have an interpretation that is well grounded and multi-dimensional, then much of the tension between the authority/obedience dialectic will be eliminated or at least reduced. That presupposes, of course, that those who make, interpret, and implement the liturgical laws and those who are meant to obey them subscribe to the same principles of interpretation.[42]

In recent years the foundational work of Ladislas Orsy on the interpretation of canon law has proven very useful in establishing rules or principles for interpreting liturgical laws.[43] His work has been applied specifically to liturgical law by a Servite canonist, John M. Huels, who completed licentiate and doctoral dissertations in canon law at The Catholic University of America under the direction of Msgr. Frederick R. McManus.[44]

Orsy's insights are drawn from the philosophical, theological, and historical disciplines, as well as from the science of canon law. He has set out fifteen rules of interpretation in succinct form, each of which he intends to be used "as a kind of legal proverb, each containing a grain of truth, but not the full truth."[45] He stresses that "none of them should be applied literally and exclusively, but each should be used with discretion and in conjunction with the others."[46] His rules of interpretation, however, concentrate more on the world of the one who formulates the text than on the world of the interpreter; in that sense they are more exegetical than hermeneutical principles. His twelfth rule affirms that meanings do not stand still but are part of an evolving universe; the commentary that follows, however, is very brief. It is in setting out the qualities of the interpreter that Orsy's remarks are more reflective of the contemporary literature on hermeneutics. As he states, "the interpreter himself does not stand still in the universal flow of history . . . He himself is developing all the time. His capacity to perceive data, understand them, judge them, will depend on how far he has progressed in this vital process of development."[47] He further states that "The broader the horizon of an interpreter, the closer his interpretation to the truth."[48] He also notes that "The interpreter who can approach the law with more sophisticated categories is more likely to find the right meaning."[49]

Although they are more exegetical than hermeneutical, several of Orsy's rules for interpretation merit comment because they have special relevance for the interpretation of liturgical laws. His second law is that the meaning of a norm depends on its literary form.[50] In recent years much attention has been given to literary forms in the study of Scripture, but the task of identifying and interpreting literary forms in canon law is a relatively new operation. There are two basic literary forms in canon law: doctrinal statements and norms of action. These two categories are usually easy to identify in liturgical law. Some liturgical laws are simply proclamations of doctrine. For example, the Rite of the Christian Initiation of Adults states in No. 27: "The sacraments of baptism, confirmation, and the eucharist are the final stage in which the elect come forward and, with their sins forgiven, are admitted into the people of God, receive the adoption of the sons of God, and are led by the Holy Spirit into the promised fullness of time and, in the eucharistic sacrifice and meal, to the banquet of the Kingdom of God."[51] That statement is simply a statement of doctrine to be interpreted on the basis of sound theological principles.

The same rite, however, contains many norms of action directing that something be said or done. They usually take one of three different forms: directive, facultative, or preceptive, each of which carries its own proper weight. A directive norm in the RCIA is found in No. 74: "The celebrant greets the candidates in a friendly manner. He speaks to them, their sponsors, and all present, pointing out the joy and happiness of the Church."[52] This norm is non-preceptive; it is simply a pastoral guideline.

A facultative norm is contained in No. 75 of the same rite which states that the celebrant may use the words printed in the text or other words in asking the candidates about their intentions.[53] A facultative norm allows a variety of options from which to choose.

A preceptive norm is contained in No. 221 of the RCIA: "If baptism is done by infusion or pouring, the celebrant takes baptismal water from the font and pours it three times on the bowed head of the candidate, baptizing him in the name of the Trinity."[54] That is an essential requirement for the proper execution of the sacrament. Directive and facultative norms may be interpreted with greater flexibility; preceptive norms must be observed with stricter fidelity.[55]

Another of Orsy's rules of interpretation which has importance in the area of liturgical law is that every norm has its own proper authority.[56] It is imperative that the interpreter be aware that not every legal utterance has equal weight. A survey of the documents that have been issued to initiate and implement liturgical renewal will show that the texts fit in various categories whose legal import is not readily grasped by those who are not specialists in canon law. Furthermore a number of the documents have not been widely publicized; hence, often through ignorance they have not been effectively implemented.

It might be noted here that in addition to the various kinds of documents that have been formally issued by the Holy See, various dicasteries also issue declarations which give an interpretation to existing laws. An authentic declaration or interpretation refers to those given with official authority as opposed to those given privately by anyone who knows the law. The Pontifical Commission for the Interpretation of the Decrees of the Second Vatican Council established by Pope Paul VI on January 3, 1966, is empowered to give such authentic interpretations of the various decrees of the Second Vatican Council and post-conciliar legislation as well. Such interpretations have the force of public law. However if a response to a question is given by one of the Roman dicasteries in the form of a rescript in a particular matter, it does not have the force of public law, but binds only the person or persons to whom it is given and in the specific matters affected by it.[57]

Responses to various liturgical questions have regularly been printed in *Notitiae*, the periodical originally issued by the

Consilium and now by the Sacred Congregation for the Sacraments and Divine Worship. These responses do not have the force of public law unless stated otherwise. When the Consilium was originally established, it was not set up as a legislative body; hence its responses to liturgical questions did not constitute part of the liturgical law of the Church. In fact the Consilium went out of its way to state that its responses in *Notitiae* were not official.[58] They were classified as *officiosa*, i.e., unofficial. The Sacred Congregation for the Sacraments and Divine Worship, however, is empowered with legislative authority. But the responses to doubts published in *Notitiae* are not legislative. Unless the decisions have been voted on and approved by a plenary meeting of the congregation, they should be considered as non-authentic interpretations, similar to those given by theologians or canonists acting as private persons. Certainly theologians and canonists may interpret liturgical law privately, with the authority warranted by their own learning. Their interpretations, however, have only the weight appropriate to the reasons on which they base their opinions. The various liturgical studies that appear in periodicals such as *Notitiae*, *Ephemerides Liturgicae*, *Worship*, *Rivista Liturgica*, and *La Maison-Dieu* would all fall under the category of non-authentic interpretations from a canonical point of view.

Surely there is a great need for liturgical legislators to clarify the legal import of their documents. Because of the current ambiguity, some documents that are relatively unimportant in content are given as much weight as those that are in fact very important. It often takes a skilled canonist to determine the legal import of texts, but at times not even the canonist can be sure of their weight. Since the documents are generally intended for those who are not in fact skilled canonists, their legal import should be quite evident. Furthermore, documents should be carefully promulgated, and there should be consistency in the mode of promulgation.

Several of Orsy's rules highlight the importance of the historical and theological contexts of liturgical norms.[59] A thorough knowledge of history includes a grasp of the cultural context of the legislator, an understanding of the evolutionary development of meanings, and a sense of the dialectical context within which some laws originate. Legal texts, including liturgical texts, are always subject to the influences of their authors: their own ideas, biases, and limitations. Likewise the ideological and sociological orientations of an age can often have an effect on the written law. In our own time, liturgical laws often seem to be the result of compromise; they are affected by diverse cultural conditions and they are frequently products of various Roman congregations, each of which has its own history, its own peculiar mode of operation, and its own members with their own unique personalities and ideological orientations.

In addition to the historical context, there is also a need to appreciate the theological context not only in which the laws were originally formulated but also the theological framework within which the interpreter operates.[60] Theology is especially important because liturgy is not simply an ordered execution of rituals, it is above all the celebration of the mystery of Christ. The competent interpreter then must have a sound grasp of both liturgical theology and pastoral theology, for the liturgy is celebrated so that Christian persons and communities might themselves appropriate the experience of the death and resurrection of Christ through the power of the Holy Spirit. Presuppositions above all in these areas are apt to shape the world of the interpreter and to have a significant effect on the hermeneutical task of bringing the interpreter's world into dialogue with the law-maker's world in order to draw out the meaning that the liturgical texts should have at the present time. As new liturgical rites were promulgated after the Council, they were regularly prefaced with theological statements which set out the context in which the rites themselves were to be interpreted and executed. However, it should be noted here that there have been important theological developments in sacramental and liturgical theology in the past decade, developments which often go beyond the theologies set out in the *praenotanda* of the various rites. Interpreters should also remember that theology is an integrated system, not a series of disjunctive tracts. Positions that one assumes in the areas of christology and ecclesiology influence one's sacramental theology and ministry. Good interpreters will be aware of their liturgical presuppositions and sensitive to the implications that their presuppositions have on their interpretations.

They will also remember that liturgical laws above all have a pastoral aim;[61] they are meant to enhance the unity, growth, and good order of the Church. However the liturgy is unlike other institutions in the Church in that its language is above all symbolic and non-discursive. Since it is concerned with the mystery of Christ, its reality can never be adequately expressed in any language, including the language of laws. Furthermore liturgy requires symbolic expressions that will vary from culture to culture, and the rites themselves will often have to be modified so as to respond to particular local needs.[62] This point was clearly asserted in the *Constitution on the Sacred Liturgy* when it stated that "pastors of souls must realize that when the liturgy is celebrated, something more is required than the mere observation of the laws governing valid and licit celebration; it is their duty to ensure also that the faithful take part fully aware of what they are doing, actively engaged in the rites, and enriched by its effects."[63]

Certainly the *Constitution on the Sacred Liturgy* and most of the liturgical documents that have been issued to implement it have been formulated in that spirit. Usually the norms that have been set down have been general and have been concerned with major issues, not with picayune details. In matters of liturgical music and liturgical art, only directives of a very general nature have been issued, and rightly so, for the creation of art, like the creation of morality, is something that cannot be legislated. Artists, architects, and musicians who agree to work for the Church should have a clear understanding of liturgical theology and the role of their proper arts in the liturgy, but talent and genius should not be stifled by legislators who are not themselves conversant with the arts. It is above all in these areas that the law should say little, once the role of the arts in the liturgy has been established. As Robert Hovda has noted, "the most valuable documents that have come out of the post-conciliar reform efforts have been those of general orientation, inspiration, and reflection on meaning, and not those that attempt to spell out details that are embarrassing in five years and crippling in fifty."[64]

Tensions over Interpretations of Liturgical Law in the United States

The significance of what has been set out in the preceding pages might be concretized by a brief discussion of two topics which have created special tensions in the United States recently because the Congregation for the Sacraments and Divine Worship interprets certain documents and practices in a way that is very different from the interpretation given by the United States Bishops' Committee on the Liturgy and the National Conference of Catholic Bishops. The first is that of communion under both kinds; the second is that of liturgical dance.

In his doctoral dissertation, John Huels sets out a clear history of the law on communion under both kinds down to the present time.[65] It is both a thorough and a careful study. In a summary article on "Trent and the Chalice: Forerunner of Vatican II?" which was published in *Worship*,[66] he points out that the Tridentine decree and doctrinal canons on the chalice neither forbid nor even disparage communion under both kinds and that a misconception about the Tridentine teaching appears in contemporary official teaching and magisterial texts; however, the misconception arises from the general historical context of both the Council of Trent and the Counter-Reformation rather than from the actual texts enacted at the Council.

Communion from the cup was one of the key concerns of the Protestant Reformers; hence many Catholics perceived the practice as symbolic of the Protestant revolt against the Catholic Church. Although many of the council fathers were opposed to any concession of the cup, the actual texts enacted by the Council authorized the pope to concede the chalice at his discretion.[67] This decree opened the way then to a total restoration of the cup, should the pope think it appropriate. Pope Pius IV did grant some indults for communion from the cup, but in the polemical context of the Post-Reformation period, subsequent popes gradually withdrew these favors.[68]

Whereas the Council of Trent relegated to the pope the decision on communion under both kinds, the Second Vatican Council in the *Constitution on the Sacred Liturgy* states that "Communion under both kinds may be conceded to both clerics and religious as well as to the laity, in the judgment of the bishop, in cases to be defined by the Apostolic See."[69] Between 1965 and 1970 liturgical law steadily increased the number of instances when communion could be received from the cup. The theological underpinnings for the practice affirmed that the sign of the eucharistic banquet and the complete fulfillment of Christ's command to eat and drink have been made clearer and more vital when communion is given under both kinds.

The current law on communion under both kinds on the general level is found in the General Instruction of the Roman Missal[70] and the instruction, *Sacramentali Communione*, issued by the Congregation for Divine Worship on June 29, 1970,[71] shortly after the promulgation of the typical edition of the Roman Missal. The latter instruction extended the competence to grant the faculty to allow the administration of communion under both kinds to all ordinaries, including vicars general and major superiors of clerical institutes; it allowed the episcopal conferences to establish normative guidelines or cases for the regions of the conference and this enlarged the authority of the ordinaries in view of the episcopal conference's responsibilities; it set out general principles governing the types of groups and the occasions for distributing communion under both kinds; and it specified that direct reception from the cup is the preferred mode of communicating. Although the instruction was generally positive in tone, it reflected a fear on the part of the Holy See of developing abuses resulting from improper administration of the cup to very large or poorly catechized groups. On the one hand, the instruction highly commended communion under both kinds because of its symbolic value and its spiritual benefits, but on the other hand it advised ordinaries not to permit the practice indiscriminately but only on specific occasions when there is a limited and homogeneous group of communicants. There is an obvious problem here: if communion under both kinds is of spiritual value for small groups, why is it not equally so for large groups? Certainly the difficulties in administering the cup to large groups are not at all insurmountable, as experience has clearly shown in this country.

Particular law on communion under both kinds was enacted in the United States by the National Conference of Catholic Bishops in 1970 and 1978. The 1970 legislation allowed communion under both kinds at Masses on days of special religious or civil significance for the people of the United States, at weekday Masses, and at Masses on Holy Thursday and at the Easter Vigil. The 1978 legislation extended communion under both kinds to Sundays and holy days. The implementation of these resolutions was left to the discretion of each ordinary. Neither in 1970 nor in 1978 were the proposals submitted to the Holy See for confirmation.[72]

In its 1980 instruction, *Inaestimabile donum*, the Sacred Congregation for the Sacraments and Divine Worship generally cited previously enacted liturgical norms, especially those on the *Constitution on the Sacred Liturgy* and the General Instruction on the Roman Missal. In No. 12 it dealt with communion under both kinds. The norm made no reference to the positive values of communion from the cup but rather concentrated on the restrictive language of *Sacramentali Communione* and introduced a new restriction: "Episcopal conferences and Ordinaries also are not to go beyond what is laid down in the present discipline." That innovation is generally interpreted as the congregation's response to the NCCB's resolution permitting communion under both kinds on Sundays and holy days; it is generally known that various members of the Curia were disturbed by the 1978 decision of the NCCB. Nonetheless the resolution is still in force; communion under both kinds may be licitly administered on Sundays and holy days in this country.[73]

The canonical reason why the resolution is still in force is that a later general law does not derogate from an earlier particular unless it explicitly states so. Furthermore *Inaestimabile donum* is really not new law; it is simply a reminder of discipline already in effect. Since the Holy See has not expressly nullified the 1978 decision of the NCCB, that resolution is still in effect. The Holy See's response to the ambiguous situation, however, will probably take the form of an apostolic indult allowing the practice of giving communion under both kinds on Sundays and holy days to continue. The simple fact is that the Holy See's interpretation of its laws and the NCCB's interpretation are radically different.[74]

The other controversial issue is that of sacred dance in the liturgy. An unsigned essay on dance in the liturgy entitled "The Religious Dance, an Expression of Spiritual Joy" was reprinted in the April–May 1982 issue of the United States Bishops' Committee on the Liturgy Newsletter. It first appeared in *Notitiae* in the June–July issue of 1975 and was translated into English in the *Canon Law Digest* for 1975 where it was rightly described as a "private" document.[75] Certainly the document was never promulgated as normative for the universal Church. It was labelled as a "qualified and authoritative" sketch and as such reflects opinion rather than official Church teaching. In no way should it be seen as superseding the Church's official documents addressed to the universal Church, although it was prefaced in *Notitiae* by the curious comment that it should be taken as an authoritative point of reference for every discussion of the matter.[76]

Both the qualitative and authoritative character of the text are highly questionable from various points of view. The essay states that in Western culture dancing is tied with love, with diversion, with profaneness, and with unbridling of the senses. When the essay expresses the opinion that dancing "cannot be introduced into liturgical celebrations of any kind whatever,"[77] it is obviously referring to this type of dancing. No one would disagree; this type of dancing would be utterly inappropriate in the liturgy even though it might be expertly executed.

In the United States, however, much popular dance is of folk origin and is associated not with unbridling of the senses but with joy, festivity, and celebration. These basic human experiences might well find appropriate expression in sacred dance for the liturgy. Indeed, dance has always been a primarily religious act for Native American Indians and Shakers; for black Americans, Latin Americans, and Southeast Asian immigrants it is both sacred and secular.

The assumption is made in the essay that "what is well received in one culture cannot be taken on by another culture."[78] The history and experience of the Church in the United States prove otherwise, since this country has never been limited to the religious traditions and expressions of a single culture. As a matter of fact, the Church in this country has traditionally welcomed and sought to make her own whatever is good in the religious heritage and expressions of all who belong to the community of faith. This attitude is surely in accord with the *Constitution on the Sacred Liturgy* which affirms that "the Church has no wish to impose a rigid uniformity in matters that do not affect the faith or the good of the whole community; rather the Church respects and fosters the genius and talents of the various races and peoples."[79] In speaking of the active participation of the people, the same document asserts that the people should be encouraged to take part not only by means of acclamations, responses, psalmody, antiphons, and songs, but also by actions, gestures, and bodily attitudes.[80] The Constitution on the Church in the Modern World speaks in the same vein: "Let the Church acknowledge new forms of art which are adapted to our age and are in keeping with the characteristics of various nations and regions. Adjusted in their mode of expression and conformed to liturgical requirements, they may be introduced into the sanctuary when they raise the mind to God."[81]

The statement on *Environment and Art in Catholic Worship* prepared by the United States Bishops' Committee on the Liturgy reflects a well-informed view when it states: "Contemporary art forms belong to the liturgical expressions of the assembly as surely as the art forms of the past. . . The assembly should be unhesitating in searching out, patronizing and using the arts and media of past and present. Because it is the action of the contemporary assembly, it has to clothe its basically traditional structures with the living flesh and blood of our times and our arts."[82] It further states that "because good liturgy is a ritual action, it is important that worship space allow for movement. Processions and interpretation through bodily movement (dance) can become meaningful parts of the liturgical celebration if done by truly competent persons in the manner that befits the total liturgical action."[83]

Ritual movement and gestures have always been part of the liturgy. Likewise the Church has a long and distinguished history as a patron of the arts, promoting the liturgical use of every fine art which fosters and expresses prayer. The Church never banned music from the liturgy simply because some music is not suited to worship. Rather she welcomes all styles of music which are of high quality and appropriate to the meaning and action of the liturgy. The same criteria of quality and appropriateness should be applied to liturgical dance. Apparently some of the officials in the Roman Curia think otherwise.

Conclusion

It is obvious that the sound interpretation of liturgical texts is a complex matter. The better interpreters will naturally be those thoroughly trained in theology, church history, canon law, liturgy, and even aesthetics. As Orsy has noted, "the broader the horizon of an interpreter, the closer his interpretation is to the truth."[84] The best interpretation will naturally be done by specialists. This points up the need then for specialists in liturgical law. Unfortunately very few canonists specialize in that area. But the typical everyday interpreters are not in fact specialists in theology, church history, canon law, liturgy and aesthetics, nor should they be expected to have detailed, academic information about the history and theology behind every norm. The typical interpreters are priests, deacons, and other ministers in the Church. This highlights the need for sound basic theological and liturgical formation, above all in seminaries and other ministerial programs, but also on diocesan and parish levels so as to provide for remedial education and for ongoing formation.

There is also the need for liturgical norms which are faithful to sound theology and which respect local customs and cultures and which are flexible enough to allow for adaptation and liturgical indigenization. Finally there is a definite need for curial officials and most canonists to familiarize themselves with the current literature on hermeneutics and its methodology, especially the work of Hans-Georg Gadamer, Paul Ricoeur, and the Americans who have contributed to the field. They must come to realize that sound interpretation of juridicial norms must go beyond mere exegesis. There is not a simple core of objective meaning behind the law which is to be discovered and then implemented. Two poles constitute the framework in which interpretation takes place: the world of the law maker and the world of the one who receives the law. It is essential that the latter world come more to the fore, framed as it is by an understanding of theology and the various sciences which inquire about human beings: cultural anthropology, psychology, philosophy, and sociology. The meaning to be discovered is not behind a text; it is out in front of the text. The text projects a world, just as Christianity itself projects a future. It is not the concern of interpretation to transport the Christian community back into the past but to realize that future for Christians living in the present. As the *Constitution on the Sacred Liturgy* affirms, the liturgy itself is the principal source for achieving that Christian transformation and realizing that Christian future.[85] If the laws are sound and the interpreters and practioners have a sound hermeneutical formation, problems and tensions in the area of liturgy will surely be diminished, and if not diminished entirely, they are more likely to be kept poised.

NOTES

1. As quoted by Gerard Noel, *The Anatomy of the Catholic Church: A Roman Catholic in an Age of Revolution* (Garden City, New York: Doubleday, 1980), p. 51.

2. Peter Coughlan, "Liturgy Modern Style," *The Tablet*, 237 (January 29, 1983) 78–79. See also Mark Searle, "Reflections on Liturgical Reform," *Worship*, 56 (1982) 414–415; Peter Hebblethwaite, *The Runaway Church: Post-Conciliar Growth or Decline* (New York: Seabury, 1975), pp. 25–41.

3. "The Bishop and Music for Worship," *Worship* 57 (1983) 37–39. Pre-conciliar American Catholicism is described at length but not

always with balance and sympathy by Garry Wills, *Bare Ruined Choirs: Doubt, Prophecy, and Radical Religion* (Garden City, New York: Doubleday, 1972), pp. 15–60.

4. Searle, p. 415.

5. Daniel Rees and Others, *Consider Your Call: A Theology of Monastic Life Today* (London: SPCK, 1978), pp. 35–36.

6. Theodor Klauser, *A Short History of the Western Liturgy* (Oxford: Oxford University Press, 1969), pp. 117–151.

7. Searle, p. 416.

8. *Notitiae*, 16 (1980) 287–296.

9. *Ibid.*, 287.

10. *Sacrosanctum Concilium*, nos. 1, 4: *AAS* 56 (1964) 97–98.

11. Searle, 413.

12. *Ibid.*, 422.

13. Thomas Kronsnicki, "A Survey Report on the Teaching and Celebration of Liturgy," CARA Seminary Forum, 3 (September, 1974) 1–8; Nathan Mitchell, "Liturgical Education in Roman Catholic Seminaries: A Report and Appraisal," *Worship*, 54 (1980) 129–157; James F. White, "The Teaching of Worship in Seminaries in Canada and the United States," *Worship*, 55 (1981) 304–332, with responses by Nathan Mitchell, pp. 319–324, and Frank C. Senn, pp. 325–332.

14. Andrew M. Greeley, "The Failures of Vatican II after Twenty Years," *America*, 146 (February 6, 1982) 86.

15. As quoted by Noel, p. 86.

16. *Sacrosanctum Concilium*, no. 26: AAS 56 (1964) 107. This sense of ownership has been greatly enhanced by the introduction of vernacular languages. See the report on the survey of the world's bishops taken by the Sacred Congregation for Sacraments and Divine Worship, *Notitiae*, no. 185 (December, 1981) 589–611.

17. *Method in Theology* (New York: Herder and Herder, 1972), p. xi.

18. Stephen Happel, "Classicist Culture and the Nature of Worship," *The Heythrop Journal*, 21 (July, 1980) 294. Happel's treatment, as well as my own, of classicist versus empiricist culture is derived from Lonergan's works, especially *Method in Theology*, pp. xi–xii, 301–302, 305–19, and *Doctrinal Pluralism* (Milwaukee: Marquette University Press, 1971), pp. 1–91.

19. See Bernard Leeming, *Principles of Sacramental Theology* (Westminster, Maryland: Newman Press, 1956), pp. 385–95.

20. Happel, p. 294.

21. Lonergan, *Method in Theology*, p. 301.

22. Happel, p. 294.

23. *Method in Theology*, p. 362. For a discussion of liturgical acculturation and indigenization, see Anscar J. Chupungco, *Cultural Adaptation of the Liturgy* (New York: Paulist Press, 1982).

24. *Sacrosanctum Concilium*, no. 10: *AAS* 56 (1964) 102.

25. See Hans Bernhard Meyer, "The Social Significance of the Liturgy," in *Politics and Liturgy*, ed. Herman Schmidt and David Power (New York: Herder and Herder, 1974), pp. 34–50.

26. Cyrille Vogel, "An Alienated Liturgy," in *Liturgy: Self-Expression of the Church*, ed. Herman Schmidt (New York: Herder and Herder, 1972), pp. 11–12.

27. Happel, p. 292.

28. See Aidan Kavanagh, *Elements of Rite* (New York: Pueblo Publishing Company, 1982), pp. 103–4.

29. See my article, "From Liturgical Reform to Christian Renewal: Unfinished Business I," *The Clergy Review*, 67 (1982) 92.

30. R. E. Palmer, *Hermeneutics: Interpretation Theory in Schleiermacher, Dilthey, Heidegger, and Gadamer* (Evanston: Northwestern University Press, 1969), pp. 3–11.

31. Basic hermeneutical presuppositions have been summarized by Sandra M. Schneiders, "The Foot Washing (John 13:1–20): An Experiment in Hermeneutics," *The Catholic Biblical Quarterly*, 43 (January, 1981) 76–80.

32. The importance of exegesis as preliminary to the hermeneutical task is set out in two articles by Raymond E. Brown, " 'And the Lord Said'? Biblical Reflections on Scripture as the Word of God," *Theological Studies*, 42 (1981) 3–19; "The Meaning of the Bible," *Theology Digest*, 28 (1980) 305–320.

33. *Interpretation Theory: Discourse and the Surplus of Meaning* (Fort Worth, Texas: Texas Christian University Press, 1976), pp. 87–88.

34. Ricoeur, pp. 31–32. See also his article, "Creativity in Language: Word, Polysemy, Metaphor," *Philosophy Today*, 17 (1973) 97–111.

35. See H.-G. Gadamer, *Truth and Method* (New York: Seabury, 1975), pp. 267–74.

36. Ricoeur, *Interpretation Theory*, p. 20.

37. See Thomas Fawcett, *The Symbolic Language of Religion* (Minneapolis: Augsburg, 1971), pp. 14–20; Nathan Mitchell, "Symbols Are Actions Not Objects: New Directions for an Old Problem," *Living Worship*, 13 (February, 1977) 1.

38. William Van Roo, *Man The Symbolizer* (Rome: Gregorian University Press, 1981), pp. 194–212.

39. See E. Marcus, "Réconcilier le devoit d'être pasteur avec celui

d'obéir," *Paroisse et Liturgie*, 47 (1965) 36–49; Walter J. Kelly, "The Authority of Liturgical Laws," *The Jurist*, 28 (1968) 397–424; Julio Manzanares Marijuan, "De obedientia et charismate in re liturgica," *Periodica*, 60 (1971) 549–572; John E. Rotelle, "Liturgy and Authority," *Worship*, 47 (1973) 514–526; Frederick R. McManus, "Liturgical Law and Difficult Cases," *Worship*, 48 (1974), 347–366.

40. Kelly, 404–405.

41. Thomas Richstatter, *Liturgical Law: New Style, New Spirit* (Chicago: Franciscan Herald Press, 1977); "Changing Styles of Liturgical Law," *The Jurist*, 38 (1978) 415–425. The work of post-conciliar commentators has been briefly reviewed by Daniel J. Ward, "Liturgy and Law," *Proceedings of the Forty-fourth Annual Convention of the Canon Law Society of America* (Washington, D.C.: Canon Law Society of America, 1983), pp. 194–195. The author's own conclusions briefly drawn need to be more carefully nuanced and give little indication of any familiarity with the more complicated hermeneutical issues.

42. John Huels, "The Interpretation of Liturgical Law," *Worship*, 55 (1981) 219–220. See also my own book, *New Liturgy, New Laws* (Collegeville: The Liturgical Press, 1980), pp. 157, 202–211.

43. "The Interpreter and His Art," *The Jurist*, 40 (1980) 27–56.

44. *The Interpretation of Liturgical Law*, Licentiate Dissertation (Washington, D.C.: The Catholic University of America, 1981); *The Interpretation of the Law on Communion under Both Kinds*, Canon Law Studies 505 (Washington, D.C.: The Catholic University of America, 1982).

45. "The Interpreter and His Art," 45.

46. *Ibid.*

47. *Ibid.*, 50.

48. *Ibid.*

49. *Ibid.*, 51.

50. *Ibid.*, 45. See also Huels, "The Interpretation of Liturgical Law," pp. 224–226.

51. *Ordo initiationis christianae adultorum* (Vatican City: Typis Polyglottis Vaticanis, 1972). Translation by the International Commission for English in the Liturgy, in *The Rites of the Catholic Church* (New York: Pueblo Publishing Company, 1976), p. 28.

52. *The Rites*, p. 41.

53. *Ibid.*

54. *Ibid.*, p. 100.

55. Huels, "The Interpretation of Liturgical Law," 225–226; Kelly, 402–403; McManus, 355.

56. "The Interpreter and His Art," 47. See also Francis G. Morrisey, "The Canonical Significance of Papal and Curial Pronouncements" (Canon Law Society of America, 1974); Seasoltz, pp. 169–181.

57. Seasoltz, pp. 176–177.

58. See the note prefixed to the section *Documentorum explanatio* in *Notitiae* 1 (1965) 137: "The solution offered has no official character, but has only the value of serving as a guideline. Any official solutions will be published where necessary by the competent authority in the *Acta Apostolicae Sedis.*"

59. "The Interpreter and His Art," 45–49. See also Huels, "The Interpretation of Liturgical Law," 229–232.

60. The interpreter's theology will affect the shape of the world in which the interpretation takes place, hence it is of great importance when discussing the hermeneutical issues.

61. Seasoltz, pp. 202–211.

62. Chupungco, pp. 42–88.

63. *Sacrosanctum Concilium,* no. 11: *AAS* 56 (1964) 103.

64. "Church Building and Renovating Problems," *Worship,* 56 (1982) 445.

65. *The Interpretation of the Law on Communion under Both Kinds.*

66. *Worship,* 56 (1982) 386–400.

67. *Decretum super petitione concessionis calicis,* session XXII, September 18, 1562: *Conciliorum Oecumenicorum Decreta,* ed. Joseph Alberigo, et al. (Bologna: Instituto per le Scienze Religiose, 1973), p. 741.

68. See G. Constant, *Concession à l'Allemagne de la Communion sous les deux espèces* (Paris: E. De Boccard, 1923), 2:522–524; Huels, "Communion under Both Kinds on Sundays: Is It Legal?" *The Jurist,* 42 (1982) 75–76.

69. *Sacrosanctum Concilium,* no. 55: *AAS* 56 (1964) 115.

70. Nos. 240–252. The original Latin text of the General Instruction accompanied the 1969 *Ordo Missae,* but it was modified in the 1975 *editio typica altera of the Missale Romanum.* The latter version carries two new norms, nos. 56h and 14, which pertain to communion under both kinds.

71. *AAS* 62 (1970) 664–666.

72. Huels, "Communion under Both Kinds: Is It Legal?" 96.

73. *Ibid.,* 101.

74. *Ibid.,* 99–105.

75. "La Danza nella Liturgia," *Notitiae,* 11 (1975) 202–205; English translation in *Canon Law Digest,* vol. 8 (Chicago: St. Mary of the Lake Seminary, 1978), pp. 78–82.

76. P. 202.
77. P. 204.
78. P. 205.
79. *Sacrosanctum Concilium*, no. 37: *AAS* 56 (1964) 110.
80. *Sacrosanctum Concilium*, no. 30: *AAS* 56 (1964) 108.
81. *Gaudium et Spes*, no. 62: *AAS* 58 (1966) 1083.
82. (Washington, D.C.: United States Catholic Conference, 1978), pp. 20–21.
83. *Ibid.*, p. 32.
84. "The Interpreter and His Art," 50.
85. *Sacrosanctum Concilium*, no. 10: *AAS* 56 (1964) 102.

4

The Sacred Liturgy: The Unfinished Task

Anscar J. Chupungco, O.S.B.

The Influence of the Classical Liturgical Movement

Vatican II's *Constitution on the Sacred Liturgy* (SC) inherited the classical features of the Liturgical Movement of the first half of this century.[1] Basing themselves on the sources of the Roman liturgy and on the scholarly studies by authors like G. Tomassi, F. Probst, A. Ebner, L. Duchesne, P. Gueranger and E. Bishop, the promoters of the movement encouraged a return to the classical form of the Roman liturgy of the fifth to the seventh century.[2] During that period the liturgy of Rome assimilated the cultural traits of the Roman people. In ritual and ceremonies as well as in the formulation of texts the liturgy breathed simplicity, sobriety and practicality.[3] It was a liturgy that expressed itself in the thought and language patterns of the people; it celebrated the mystery of Christ in Roman cultural patterns.

The Roman sacramentaries, especially the Veronese, witness to the sobriety and directness of prayer texts: God is addressed simply as *Deus*, with restrained use of adjectives; the mystery of Christ's birth is veiled with sobriety that approaches reserve: "He deigned to share our human nature."[4] Picturesque or sentimental language is totally ignored. No mention is made of the little Lord Jesus in swaddling clothes on the cold winter night. The Roman prayer text lacks the dramatic language of later euchological compositions. Unlike the *Exultet*, the Gregorian Collect simply states that the glory of the resurrection has enlightened the Easter night.[5] Pentecost is seen not as a dramatic event, but as the instruction of the faithful by the Holy Spirit.[6]

The *Ordo Romanus I* of the seventh century is a detailed description of the papal Mass in the basilica of Saint Mary Major.[7] There the sense of practicality, as opposed to the symbolic gestures, permeates the celebration. The entrance, offertory and communion songs, for example, have the function of accompanying the rite. The altar is prepared, not before the Mass, but at the moment the gifts are gathered, thus showing the functional nature of the altar as eucharistic table.[8] The rite of washing the hands is in connection with the gathering of gifts and lacks any symbolic significance. Although the entrance rite possesses an imperial grandeur, influenced no doubt by the imperial court, the rest of the celebration is simple, sober and almost severe in structure.[9] Movements are measured and reduced to the minimum necessary. Orderliness is an essential feature of the Roman celebration. To avoid crowding at communion, the Pope distributed holy communion only to persons who received the privilege, a practice similar to the issuing of communion tickets at papal Masses.

When this classical form of the Roman liturgy migrated to the Franco-Germanic territory in the eighth century, it became immediately obvious that such simplicity, brevity and sobriety could not satisfy the northerners' sense of drama, symbolic ritual and sentimental expression.[10] Before long the gap between liturgy and culture was bridged by the assimilation of their religious culture. Apologies were introduced in the imported liturgy, prayer texts were expanded, rituals were enriched with more rubrics on genuflections, signs of the cross, incensations and use of candles.[11] It was during this period that the Roman liturgy became a hybrid of Roman and Franco-Germanic elements. It was a liturgy that in its own way answered the cultural needs of the northerners. When this hybrid form returned to Rome in the tenth century, it overthrew the previous classical form.[12] Later commentators on the Roman

Mass who were not aware of the historical background would often speak of the "sensuousness of the Roman rite."[13]

The promoters of the Liturgical Movement aimed at recovering the classical form by cleansing it of its Franco-Germanic accretions. And this is the mentality that they passed onto the framers of Vatican II's *Constitution on the Sacred Liturgy.* SC 21 says liturgical elements subject to change "not only may but ought to be changed with the passing of time, if features have by chance crept in which are less harmonious with the intimate nature of the liturgy, or if existing elements have grown less functional. In this restoration, both texts and rites should be drawn up so that they express more clearly the holy things which they signify."[14] SC 34 adds that the "rites should be distinguished by a noble simplicity; they should be short, clear and unencumbered by useless repetitions; they should be within the people's power of comprehension, and normally should not require much explanation."[15] SC 50 asks that the rites of the Mass "be simplified, while due care is taken to preserve their substance. Elements which, with the passage of time, came to be duplicated, or were added with but little advantage, are now to be discarded."[16]

What is SC's motive for bringing the Roman liturgy back to its classical form? The articles cited above give conscious and active participation as a basic reason: "Christian people, as far as possible, should be able to understand them (texts and rites) with ease and to take part in them fully, actively and as befits a community."[17] "They (the rites) should be within the people's powers of comprehension, and normally should not require much explanation."[18] And the meaning and connection of the parts of the Mass should be more clearly shown, so that "devout and active participation by the faithful can be more easily achieved."[19]

On the basis of SC 37–40, however, it can be suggested that there is another motive which is equally important, although it is not immediately linked to SC's bid for classical restoration. These articles constitute the section on "the norms for adapting the liturgy to the genius and traditions of people,"[20] in other words the various contemporary cultures. The return to classical form, to simplicity, sobriety and practicality, to the essential transparency of the Roman liturgy, is not for the purpose of engaging in archeological recovery or romantic historicism, but of facilitating the adaptation of the Roman liturgy to various cultures.[21]

A hybrid Franco-Germanic Roman liturgy can hardly assimilate contemporary cultural elements without becoming bloated and incomprehensible. But if it is restored to its classical state, it can easily lend itself to new modifications through cultural assimilation. What the Franco-Germanic churches did to the classical Roman liturgy in the eighth century can and should be done by contemporary local Churches throughout the world. The Roman genius of simplicity, sobriety and practicality is not shared by every culture, including that of modern Rome. If no attempt is made to bridge the gap between the Roman classical liturgy and today's classical expressions, can Vatican II's program of conscious, intelligent and active participation be achieved? Unless the liturgy embodies the thought and language patterns and cultural forms with which the people can identify themselves, will they ever claim it as their own? If we accept as a fact that there existed a Franco-Germanic Roman liturgy in the past, should we not accept the possibility of various Roman liturgies of the future? A North American Roman liturgy, a black Roman liturgy, an Hispano-American Roman liturgy as well as Third-World Roman liturgies should have as equal a chance as the Franco-Germanic Roman Liturgy.

Liturgical Adaptation According to SC 37–40

Articles 37–40 of SC contain the norms for adapting the Roman liturgy to contemporary cultures. They will be better appreciated if they are read in the context of the other articles of SC. While SC 21, 34 and 50 clear the ground for adaptation by invoking a return to the classical features of the Roman liturgy, particularly SC 23, offer procedural principles. SC 23 speaks of retention of sound tradition and, at the same time, of openness to legitimate progress. To this effect, it requires that each part of the liturgy that is to be revised should be subjected to a theological, historical and pastoral investigation. Furthermore, recent liturgical reforms and indults should be taken into account, and both the common good of the Church and the historical evolution of liturgical forms should be guaranteed when instituting liturgical changes.[22] Adaptation to cultures is the *terminus ad quem*, but this would be impossible to achieve in a homogeneous way, if the *terminus a quo* or the historical and theological meaning of the rite is not taken into consideration.

To adapt to contemporary idiom the famous Christmas prayer *Deus, qui humanae substantiae dignitatem*, it is imperative to know who composed it and what is its underlying theological message. Should one not take into account that the prayer was composed by Pope Leo the Great in defense of human dignity against Manicheans, one could translate *dignitas* as weakness, as ICEL in fact does, or *dignatus est* as "he humbled himself," as we find in the Book of Common Prayer. Such translations are surely not against faith, indeed they are more biblical, but they are in opposition to Pope Leo's theology of Christmas. According to Pope Leo what the Word assumed in the Incarnation was human dignity and he considered it worthy of his concern.[23]

The historical background of the rites should also be kept in mind, otherwise there can be a danger of misinterpreting them. During the Middle Ages lack of historical basis led to the dramatic shift from giving a kiss to administering a slap on the cheek of the newly confirmed. The bishop's fatherly greeting of peace became a knighting ceremony, thus making the newly confirmed a soldier of Christ.[24] It was also lack of historical perspective that led Amalar of Metz and later liturgical commentators, including Pope Innocent III, to interpret the rites of the Mass in the context of the Passion narrative.[25] An extreme example of such interpretations is that the priest's washing of hands recalls Pilate's gesture before he condemned Jesus to the cross.[26] As far down as the scholastic period the rite of commingling was interpreted as the resurrection of Jesus or the reunion of his body and blood which are symbolically separated in sacrifice in the separate consecration of bread and wine.[27]

In the process of adaptation such mistakes should not be repeated. This explains SC's insistence on a thorough theological and historical investigation of the liturgy. And it is only with a clear understanding of the *terminus a quo* of liturgical adaptation that we can begin to move towards the *terminus ad quem* proposed by SC 37–40.

SC 37 lays down the general principles of adaptation. It applies to the liturgy Pope Pius XII's encyclical letter *Summi Pontificatus* which it cites extensively.[28] In the liturgy the Church has no wish to impose a rigid uniformity in the matters which do not touch the faith and the good of the whole Church. Research on Council proceedings yields an encouraging result for local Churches that do not fall in the category of missions. The liturgical pluralism advocated by SC 37 is not primarily of a missionary bent, but of the cultural nature.[29] It focuses its attention on the genius and talents of the various races and peoples and on their way of life. In other words, on elements which constitute culture. These, says SC 37, the Church "sometimes in fact admits into the liturgy itself." It would seem then that when a given culture differs from the cultural framework of the Roman liturgy in thought, language and ritual pattern, adaptation is justified, regardless of whether the local Church is in the mission land or not. While SC 4 declares that the council admits liturgical pluralism with respect to other existing liturgical rites in both East and West, SC 37 goes further. It envisages new liturgies, based on the Roman, which will correspond more faithfully to the culture and traditions of various races and peoples.

What are the conditions for admitting cultural elements into the liturgy? One is negative: "Anything that is not indissolubly bound up with superstition and error."[30] The other is positive: "As long as they harmonize with the true and authentic spirit of the liturgy."[31] To this one may add the requirement of SC 40 that adaptation should be useful or necessary, otherwise it could lead to romanticism, archeologism, exhibitionism or plain gimmickry. SC 37 offers the broadest possible margin: anything that can be salvaged from superstition and error, and as long as it harmonizes with the true and authentic liturgical spirit.[32] SC 38 specifies who are to benefit from liturgical adaptation: the different assemblies, regions and peoples.[33] In other words, every cultural group, especially, though not exclusively, in the missions. SC 39 enumerates the areas of adaptation. These are the sacraments, sacramentals, liturgical language, sacred music and art.[34]

At this point it may be useful to note that both SC 38 and 39 envisage adaptation as local applications of the possible changes or modifications of the Roman liturgy as provided for in the new liturgical books. The introduction to these books includes a section which specifies the cases of adaptation that may be carried out by the bishops' conferences.[35] SC 40, on the other hand, deals with cases of adaptation that are not foreseen by the liturgical books. It is up to the bishops' conference to "carefully and prudently consider which elements from the traditions and culture of individual peoples might appropriately be admitted into divine worship."[36] Adaptations of this kind require the consent of the Holy See after the preliminary experiments over a determined period of time among certain groups suited for the purpose. So much for the question of procedure. What engages our attention is the formulation of the principles of adaptation derived from SC, especially articles 37–40. Indeed these articles raise three basic questions which can lead to the formulation of principles. Which cultural elements may be admitted into the liturgy? What is meant by the true and authentic spirit of the liturgy? And how do cultural elements harmonize with that spirit?

The Cultural Aspects of Liturgical Adaptation

Without entering into a detailed discussion of culture, suffice it to say that its principal elements are the people's thought and language patterns, their values and beliefs, their rituals and traditions, and their literature and artistic expressions. Underlying all this is the people's genius or their natural, spontaneous response to a given reality. Such a response is expressed, according to the pattern specific to a cultural group, in language, rituals, traditions and the arts. Cultural adaptation requires therefore not only a knowledge of the genius of the Roman liturgy, the *terminus a quo*, but also of the contemporary culture in question, the *terminus ad quem.* Since the liturgy consists principally of words and action or text and ritual, adaptation will occupy itself with the question of language and rites, and how these can be introduced in the Roman liturgy as substitutes or explanations of its parts.

The adaptation of the Roman euchology or prayer formula would imply a kind of dynamic translation.[37] In the fifth to the seventh century the message of the Roman euchology was addressed to the Roman assembly with the simplicity, sobriety, directness and theological precision of the Latin language. Today the same message will have to be communicated to culturally distinct assemblies according to their thought and language patterns and their idiomatic expressions. This may be accomplished by substituting the classical Roman features with the linguistic traits of the local culture. The Roman simplicity and sobriety may have to give way to a more elaborate and dramatic formulation.[38] Its directness may have to yield to a round-about manner of speaking, and its highly intellectual language may have to be laid aside in favor of symbolic and picturesque language that appeals more to the senses and sentiments than to the intellect. Thus, depending on the culture of the assembly, the Collect of Pentecost Sunday could visualize that event in a dramatic language that departs from the sober and measured language of the original text.

Dynamic translation may also imply substitution of the Roman mode of response to external factors as well as of the values found in the euchology. The Leonine Collect of Christmas, mentioned above, expresses a response of contemplative admiration (*mirabiliter, mirabilius*) for God's work of creation and redemption. Another culture with the propensity to efficiency and action could respond differently to the same deed of God. While the original text says, "You created human dignity wonderfully and redeemed it even more wonderfully," the ICEL text substitutes this contemplative admiration with action: "We praise you for creating man, and still more for restoring him in Christ."[39] Still another cultural group may respond to the same reality according to its traditional attitudes toward God who is both loving and merciful: "In love you created man, in mercy you redeemed him."[40] In both cases the original message is not lost, but conveyed according to the culture's mode of response to God's work of creation and redemption.

Human values, especially those highly cherished by a culture, could play a decisive role in the adaptation of euchological formulas. In societies where hospitality, for example, is greatly valued, figures of speech, maxims and proverbs on hospitality could be employed to express the message of the Roman euchology. For example, the Leonine Christmas Collect which speaks of the sharing of the Son of God in our humanity and of our sharing in his divinity could be expressed in terms of hospitality on the part of man who considers the Incarnate Word as full member of the human family or hospitality on the part of God who welcomes man into his bosom.[41]

Another linguistic element that deserves special consideration is idiomatic expressions. These are hardly translatable, because they grow from the thought and language patterns proper to each culture. They evoke images and values that can be grasped and appreciated only by those who belong to the culture. The use of such expressions could culturally enrich euchology inasmuch as they evoke cultural settings that are familiar to the listeners. They could also allow the assembly to identify itself culturally with the euchological text, because this speaks the language of the assembly, follows its pattern of thought and speech, and evokes the realities of its life.[42]

The action or ritual aspect of the liturgy includes gestures and material elements which, in the course of the celebration, become the symbol of the presence of Christ and his mystery. Since the liturgy is essentially performative, action takes precedence over material elements.[43] In other words, these become living symbols in the liturgy because of the action performed over them with or without the accompaniment of words. Water, for example, is not a baptismal symbol unless the minister, who recites the words, pours it on the candidate; bread and wine are not eucharistic symbols if the action of the eucharistic prayer is not performed over them; oil is not a sacramental symbol if it is not applied on the sick person.[44] Cultural adaptation should thus take into account the symbolic nature and function of rituals. Elements taken from contemporary cultures should become symbols of the mystery which the liturgy celebrates. Because they are meant to be symbols, they should possess a certain connaturality with the Christian mystery, they should lend themselves to Christian interpretation and adequately convey the liturgical message.

The Greco-Roman culture and afterwards the Franco-Germanic have had notable influence on the formation of the Roman liturgy. Today elements from those cultures survive especially in the so-called explanatory rites of sacramental celebrations. The liturgy of infant baptism has preserved anointing with chrism as a symbol of priesthood, the white garment as a symbol of Christian dignity conferred by baptism, and the lighted candle as a symbol of Christian faith which the newly baptized must keep burning. These three symbols originated at different centuries under different conditions. Tertullian was the first to speak of baptismal anointing which he compared to the priestly anointing of Aaron by Moses.[45] Almost two centuries later Ambrose of Milan would give it a more cultural setting. To the newly baptized he declared: "You have been anointed as an athlete of Christ."[46] Greek and Roman athletes were massaged with oil before combat; at baptism the Christian too was anointed with oil to do battle for Christ especially in times of persecution. It is probable that baptismal anointing has been borrowed from the athletic practice of the Greco-Roman world and given a Christian meaning by the Fathers of the Church. The use of a white garment and the procession with lighted candles appeared in the fourth century.[47] The white garment could have originated from the Roman toga worn by citizens as a sign of their dignity, whence the meaning it has today in baptism. The initiates to the cult of Mithras were also vested in white.[48] The procession with lighted candles, on the other hand, could have been derived from the practice of carrying candles during imperial processions.[49] Ambrose described in one of his homilies how the neophytes, dressed in white and with candles burning in their hands, processed toward the altar to the great admiration and envy of angels.[50]

Of interest to cultural adaptation is a curious practice mentioned by Hippolytus of Rome.[51] During their first holy communion the neophytes received a mixed drink of milk and honey. The Romans also gave the drink to newly born infants both as a sign of welcome to the family and as a means of protecting them from evil powers. Hippolytus, however, explained it as a symbol of the neophyte's entry to the land flowing with milk and honey, after crossing the Jordan or the water of baptism.[52]

These examples indicate that the explanatory rites of sacramental celebrations are culturally bound. They were introduced into the liturgy in order to explain the meaning of the celebration through gestures and symbols of the culture. And because culture changes from age to age and from place to place, the ritual adaptation of the liturgy did not come to an end with the Greco-Romans. In the eighth century, the Franco-Germanic people introduced their own gestures and symbols. And the process of liturgical evolution went on during the Middle Ages and down to the Baroque period. The reform of Vatican II, far from putting an end to such an evolution, invites contemporary cultures to contribute to the process of liturgical adaptation.

In this connection a few questions can be raised. Besides the explanatory rites, what other elements of the Roman liturgy are culturally bound? Which of these elements may be substituted with contemporary ones? If certain elements, especially those of biblical origin, are irreplaceable, is it advisable to give them new explanatory rites?

True and Authentic Spirit of the Liturgy

What is meant by the liturgy's true and authentic spirit? In the process of cultural adaptation which elements of the liturgy should be kept intact, besides faith and the good of the whole Church? While not wishing to enter into a detailed discussion of such elements, the following principles are briefly discussed.

SC 33 declares that "the liturgy is above all things the worship of the divine majesty."[53] This principle dictates the essential condition and sets the limits of adaptation. Liturgical celebration cannot be anything less than an act of worship. That is why, if elements from culture such as dramatic expressions are introduced into the liturgy, they will have to become expressions of worship and not mere theatrical display. They should, in the words of SC 21, "express clearly the holy things which they signify."[54] Even the catechetical aspect of the liturgy should be viewed against this backdrop. For the liturgy is not a classroom catechesis, but presupposes previous instruction in the faith and in the mystery of Christ. It instructs not by catechizing but by celebrating; it does not infuse new knowledge, but deepens what the assembly already possesses.

The center of every liturgical celebration is Christ and his paschal mystery. This principle may create problems in places where divine attributes such as the mercy of God or the role of angels and saints have a prominent place in religious culture. The liturgy, it should be noted, does not celebrate divine attributes or theological doctrines, but the deed of God in Christ from the Incarnation to the sending of the Holy Spirit. At the heart of this divine activity is the paschal mystery. That is why, SC 104 says that on the feast of saints the Church "proclaims the paschal mystery as achieved in the saints who have suffered and been glorified with Christ."[55] This explains why the mystery of faith proclaimed by the Church at every liturgical celebration, whether it be Christmas, Pentecost or solemnity of a saint, is always the paschal mystery.

Equally important is the primacy of God's written Word. "Sacred Scripture," says SC 24, "is of paramount importance in the celebration of the liturgy." There is no need to discuss here the impropriety of substituting the Word of God with other literature, even if this be a patristic, papal or conciliar document. Nor is there a need to enter into the question of sacred books of other religions and their place in Christian liturgy. But it may be useful to mention that the primacy of God's Word implies, as SC 24 states, that "prayers, collects and liturgical songs are scriptural in their inspiration, and it is from Scripture that actions and signs derive their meaning." Although Roman collects and the majority of prefaces avoid direct scriptural quotations because of their literary *cursus* or rhythmic measure, they are steeped in biblical themes.[56] Gallican prayer formulas, on the contrary, quote the Scripture verbatim.[57] Although the adaptation of liturgical texts involves the use of literary forms proper to the culture, the content or theme cannot be anything but scriptural or at least scripturally bound.

Active participation is another important principle of liturgical adaptation. The classical Liturgical Movement and Vatican II greatly promoted it, and today its extent cannot be equalled by the active pariticpation spoken of by the Roman Order of Mass in the seventh century. SC 28 has insisted however that "in liturgical celebrations, whether as a minister or as one of the faithful, each person should perform his role by doing solely and totally what the nature of things and liturgical norms require of him." Good order is a requirement of every community celebration. And in the liturgy good order consists essentially of the distinction between the president of the assembly and the assembly itself. However, the delineation of roles, whether of the president, the ministers or the assembly, is subject to both theological and cultural influences. History itself witnesses to the evolution of liturgical roles, such as the recitation of the eucharistic prayer and the ministry of homily which were, once upon a time, reserved to the bishop, and the Lord's Prayer which was recited by the president of the assembly alone. Cultural adaptation implies a reassessment of liturgical roles and ministries in the light of both the liturgical tradition and the cultural patterns in community participation.

Much has been written on symbol in the liturgy. There is no need to repeat here what authors like A. Nocent, E. Lengeling, P. Fink and J. Gelineau have said on the subject.[58] Nor is there a need to discuss the principle enunciated by SC 21 that "the liturgy is made up of unchangeable elements divinely instituted, and elements subject to change." Earlier in this chapter the explanatory rites and other similar signs and gestures were proposed as possible areas of cultural adaptation. A few other considerations of a practical nature could be added here. In introducing new symbols in the liturgy, care should be taken that they possess a certain connaturality with Christian worship and that they can be made to convey the liturgical message. Their cultural origin should also be taken into account. What is relevant to one culture may smack of artificiality to another and thus become a cultural imposition. Similarly the revival of extinct symbols may lead to romantic historicism or archeologism.

Contemporary symbols, however, should be integrated in the liturgical ambit in such a way that they can lead the assembly to the mystery which is being celebrated. Lack of integration will keep the new symbols as a separate unit that evokes its cultural origin but does not communicate the liturgical message. And finally, symbols should be fully "performed" (symbols are in the category of activities) and should not be reduced to simple tokens or remnants, such as a few drops of baptismal water, a trace of unperfumed chrism and eucharistic wafer at holy communion. Even before proposing new symbols, it might not be a bad idea to review how we perform existing symbols. Is holy communion what contemporary culture means by community meal? Does baptismal water truly wash? Incidentally, immersion is preferred by the new rite of infant baptism.[59] Is baptismal anointing realistic enough? Tertullian spoke of a generous amount of oil used in baptismal anointing. "The oil," he said, "runs down our bodies."[60] The same question can be raised regarding other liturgical symbols: the laying on of hands at the rite of reconciliation, the sign of peace, procession on Palm Sunday, fire on Easter vigil, etc. Symbols should be reviewed in the light of their historical and theological meaning as well as their cultural relevance. Today, what does a liturgical procession mean and how should it be performed? And how about gestures like genuflecting, raising and laying on of hands, clapping of hands and swaying of the body? Or material elements like fire and incense, perfume and flowers, and water and oil?

The Process of Liturgical Adaptation

Having seen both the cultural and the theological principles of adaptation, we turn our attention to the third question raised in connection with SC 37, namely how to harmonize cultural elements with the true and authentic spirit of the liturgy. Some authors would speak here of the process of purification.[61] It means that cultural elements are divested of features which are contrary to faith and are made to assume the role of a liturgical symbol. The question, however, is how this can be concretely achieved. The history of adaptation shows that during the patristic period cultural elements assumed in the liturgy were reinterpreted in the light of salvation history. Biblical typology was often employed, no doubt in order to incorporate cultural elements into the framework of salvation history. SC 24 approves of this patristic method when it says that "it is from Scripture that actions and signs derived their meaning."

A few examples will help to illustrate this point. Tertullian, who was a Latin jurist by profession before his conversion, employed juridical terms to explain Christian baptism. He called the rite of renunciation *eieratio*, a legal term which meant adjuration of contract or partnership; the profession of faith before baptism he termed *sacramenti testatio* which meant the soldier's oath of allegiance to the emperor.[62] After baptism the bishop received the neophyte into the community. Tertullian called this act *susceptio*, again a legal term which indicated that the *paterfamilias* officially recognized a newly born infant as his.[63]

A striking example of the use of terms that had sociopolitical connotations is found in the three ordination prayers in the sixth-century Sacramentary of Verona. Two of these prayers, one for the presbyter, the other for the deacon, are still used today. In all three prayers the words *dignitas, gradus* and *honor* are repeatedly used.[64] These words referred to the rank and career of civil servants who were promoted by stages.[65] The application of such words to clerics had not been a fruitful one, especially as regards the deacon who, according to the prayer, could hope to be promoted to the higher ranks, if he proved himself faithful to his third-class ministry. Until the reform of Paul VI the diaconate was considered as a transitional phase in the hierarchical ministry.[66] Even today one can still hear such expressions as ecclesiastical career. But the redeeming value of these prayers lies in their doctrine that ecclesiastical dignity and honor come from God and must be used for his service.

Biblical typology was used by the Fathers to explain other

elements borrowed from culture. Tertullian, as we have seen, used an Old Testament type to show the meaning of baptismal anointing. As Aaron was anointed priest by Moses, so the Christian is also anointed priest at baptism. Hippolytus spoke of the entry of the Israelites to the land flowing with milk and honey as the type of the rite of giving the mixed drink of milk and honey to neophytes during their first holy communion. The prayer of episcopal ordination mentioned above also makes use of biblical typology. The text alludes to the vestments of Old Testament high priests in an effort to justify the bishop's use of imperial robes. The glorious garb of the bishop, the *gloria pontificalis,* prefigured by that of the high priest, manifests the interior splendor, *splendor animorum,* of the one who wears it.[67]

These examples show how the Church Fathers "purified" cultural elements, both linguistic and ritual, by reinterpreting them in the light of Christian revelation. By doing this they allowed culture to convey to their contemporaries what would have otherwise remained alien or simply incomprehensible. All this shows a daring spirit and an inventiveness which put later generations to embarrassment. Anointing the whole body with oil and offering milk and honey to neophytes during holy communion would probably be an object of derision or a cause of suspension from ministry, but they reveal the courage of a youthful Church. For the purpose of creating a living liturgy, a liturgy in which people saw and touched the mystery of Christ depicted by their own culture, nothing was so profane that it could not express the sacred, and nothing was so sacred that it could not be expressed by the profane. Many centuries have passed, but the Church has not forgotten.

Conclusion

Twenty years ago Vatican II's *Constitution on the Sacred Liturgy,* especially articles 37–40, tried to recapture the valor of the past ages. The adaptation of the liturgy to various cultures and traditions was one of its major concerns. And rightly so, for it is the surest way of promoting genuine liturgical life in the local churches throughout the world. As long as the liturgy is untouched by the culture of the people, it will remain alien, and the mystery it bears can penetrate the depths of their heart and spirit only with the greatest difficulty. And so the *Constitution on the Sacred Liturgy* has set up an agenda, the on-going agenda of the liturgical adaptation, so that the Church may continually renew herself and stay young, creative and daring like her eternal Bridegroom and the Holy Spirit that inspires and moves her.[68]

NOTES

1. *Sacrosanctum Concilium*, n. 34: AAS 56 (1964) p. 109.
2. B. Neunheuser, *Storia della liturgia attraverso le Epoche Culturali*, Rome 1973, pp. 150–155.
3. E. Bishop, *Liturgia Historica*, Oxford 1918, p. 12.
4. L. Mohlberg (ed.), *Sacramentarium Veronense*, n. 1239, Rome 1978, p. 157.
5. J. Deshusses (ed.), *Le Sacramentaire Gregorien*, n. 377, Fribourg 1971, p. 189.
6. *Ibid.*, 227.
7. M. Andrieu (ed.), *Les Ordines Romani du Haut Moyen Age*, Louvain 1971, II, pp. 71–72.
8. *Ibid.*, p. 90.
9. *Ibid.*, pp. 80–82; J. Jungmann, *The Early Liturgy*, London 1966, pp. 131–133.
10. B. Neunheuser, *op. cit.*, pp. 93, 95–96.
11. J. Jungmann, *The Mass of the Roman Rite*, London 1959, pp. 58–59.
12. *Ibid.*, pp. 71–74.
13. O. B. Hardison Jr., *Christian Rite and Christian Drama in the Middle Ages*, Baltimore 1965, pp. 77–79.
14. AAS 56 (1964) pp. 105–106.
15. *Ibid.*, p. 109.
16. *Ibid.*, p. 114.
17. SC n. 21, p. 106.
18. SC n. 34, p. 109.
19. *Ibid.*, p. 114.
20. *Ibid.*, p. 110.
21. B. Neunheuser, "*Le Riforme della Liturgia Romana: Storia e Caratteristiche*," in: S. Marsili (ed.), *Anàmnesis*, Turin 1978, II, p. 253.

22. AAS 56 (1904) p. 106.

23. A. Chupungco, "The English Translation of the Latin Liturgy," in: *Notitiae* 187 (1982) p. 97.

24. A. Andrieu (ed.), *Le Pontifical Romain au Moyen Age: Le Pontifical de Guillaume Durand*, Vatican City 1940, pp. 334, 450.

25. J. M. Hanseens (ed.), *Amalarii episcopi opera liturgia omnia*, Vatican City 1958, II, pp. 330, 345–346; Innocent III, *De sacro altaris mysterio* PL 217, columns 773–914.

26. J. M. Hanseens (ed.), *op. cit.*

27. *Summa Theologica*, III, q. 83, ad 5.

28. AAS 31 (1939) p. 429.

29. B. Neunheuser, "*Le Riforme della Liturgia Romana: Storia e Caratteristiche*," in: S. Marsili (ed.), *Anàmnesis*, Turin 1978, II, p. 253.

30. AAS 56 (1964) p. 110.

31. *Ibid.*

32. *Ibid.*

33. *Ibid.*

34. *Ibid.*

35. *Ordo Initiationis Christianae Adultorum*, Vatican City 1972, pp. 29–30; *Ordo Baptismi Parvulorum*, Vatican City 1973, pp. 12, 20; *Ordo Confirmationis*, Vatican City 1973, pp. 19, 21; *Missale Romanum*, Vatican City 1975, pp. 32, 33, 42, 46, 67, 70, 76, 81, 83, 86, 90, 106; *Ordo Lectionum Missae*, Vatican City 1981, XXXVI, XLVI; *Ordo Poenitantiae*, Vatican City 1974, p. 24; *Ordo Unctionis Infirmorum Eorumque Pastoralis Curae*, Vatican City 1975, pp. 21–22; *Ordo Celebrandi Matrimonium*, Vatican City 1972, p. 10.

36. AAS 56 (1964) p. 111.

37. *Consilium ad Exsequendam Constitutionem de Sacra Liturgia, Instructio ad Praeses Conferentiarum Episcoporum et Commissionum Liturgicarum de quibusdam Normis circa Interpretationes Populares Textuum Liturgicorum pro Celebratione cum Populo*, January 25, 1969, n. 7.

38. A. Chupungco, *Towards A Filipino Liturgy*, Manila 1976, pp. 92–93.

39. ICEL, *The Roman Missal*, Washington 1973, part two (no pagination).

40. This translation is inspired by the English rendition of the second preface for weekdays.

41. Regional Committee for Tagalog in the Liturgy, *Aklat ng Pagmimisa sa Roma*, Manila 1981, p. 160.

42. Archbishop R. Vidal, "Notes on the Tagalog Translation of the Roman Missal," in: *Notitiae* 191–192 (1982), pp. 368–369, 372.

43. V. Turner, "Ritual, Tribal and Catholic," in: *Worship* 50 (1976) p. 506; Tad Guzie, *The Book of Sacramental Basics,* Ramsey 1981, pp. 53, 57, 66.

44. Tad Guzie, *op. cit.,* pp. 24–37; cf. also N. Mitchell, *Cult and Controversy: The Worship of the Eucharist outside Mass,* New York 1982, pp. 396–387.

45. R. Refonle (ed.), *De Baptismo,* n. 7; in *Source Chrétien* (1952) p. 76.

46. B. Botte (ed.), *De Sacramentis I,* n. 4; in *Source Chrétien* 25 bis (1961) p. 62.

47. St. Gregory Nazianzus, "*De sancto Pascha II*" PG XXXVI, columns 425 and 644; St. Gregory of Nyssa, "*De sancto Pascha IV,*" PG XLVI, column 681.

48. E. Yarnold, "Baptism and Pagan Mysteries in the Fourth Century," in: *The Heythrop Journal* 13 (1974) p. 253.

49. J. Jungmann, *The Early Liturgy,* pp. 132–133.

50. *De Mysteriis,* 8, 43; *De Sacramentis IV,* 2, 5.

51. B. Botte (ed.), *La Tradition Apostolique de Saint Hippolyte,* Münster 1963, n. 21, pp. 56–59.

52. *Ibid.,* pp. 56–57.

53. AAS 56 (1964) p. 108.

54. *Ibid.,* p. 106.

55. *Ordo Lectionum Missae,* Vatican City 1981, p. XVIII.

56. A. Chupungco, "The English Translation of the Latin Liturgy," in: *Notitiae* 187 (1982), p. 93.

57. *Ibid.*

58. A. Nocent, "*The Liturgical Year,*" Collegeville 1977, 4 volumes; J. Gelineau, "The Symbols of Christian Initiation," in: W. Reedy (ed.), *Becoming a Catholic Christian,* New York 1979, pp. 190–196.

59. *Ordo Initiationis Christianae Adultorum,* Vatican City 1972, pp. 22, 92, 108; *Ordo Baptismi Parvulorum,* Vatican City 1973, pp. 11, 19, 32, 44, 54, 64.

60. *De Baptismo* 7, *op cit.,* p. 76.

61. X. Scumois, "*Norme per adattare la liturgia al carattere ed alle tradizioni dei diversi popoli,*" in: V. Joannes (ed.), *Commento alla Costituzione sulla Liturgia,* Brescia 1965, pp. 75–109.

62. *De Spectaculis* XXIV, 2–3, CCL I (1954) p. 248.

63. *De Corona* III, 3, CCL II (1954) pp. 1042–1043.

64. L. Mohlberg (ed.), *Sacramentarium Veronense,* nn. 118–122.

65. D. Power, *Ministers of Christ and His Church,* London 1969, pp. 58–73.

66. Pope Paul VI, "*Pontificalis Romani Recognitio,*" June 18, 1968, AAS 60 (1968) p. 372.

67. L. Mohlberg, *op. cit.*

68. Cardinal J. Knox, "*Relatio de laboribus et inceptis Sacrae Congregationis pro Cultu divino et Synodum Episcoporum* 1974," in: *Notitiae* 10 (1974) pp. 355–356.

5
The Sacred Liturgy: Toward the Fullness of Human Existence

Theresa F. Koernke, I.H.M.

The Church has existed in time before us and will continue beyond us. This sinful and holy Church has to do with the presence of God in our flesh, in the time of our human history. It has to do with the truth of faith at whose mention a vast majority of Catholics genuflected on countless noon-day play-fields: THE WORD WAS MADE FLESH AND DWELLS AMONG US. It is our faith that the humanity of Jesus was created and sanctified in a manner so profound that what has transpired in the flesh of Jesus forms the basis of our hope as human beings. Or, to put it another way: the conclusion of our contemplation over the Mystery of Christ is precisely not anxiety over the great abyss between us and God, nor is it denial of our sinfulness or indifference to it. The conclusion to be drawn from the contemplation on the life, cross and resurrection, and the bestowal of the Spirit upon this Church is that nothing can separate us from the Creator whom we have been taught to address as Abba.

To reflect upon the topic: "The Sacred Liturgy: Toward the Fullness of Human Existence" is to reflect upon Spirituality: that over-all orientation of our lives which is grounded upon the revelation of God in the human community. It is in the light of this truth of faith that we might dare to speak of Liturgy as key factor in our journey toward the fullness of human existence.

Various things have occurred in the history of the Great Church (as the Fathers loved to call it), some of which can be said to have been deeper graspings of the experience of the Triune God revealed in Jesus of Nazareth. And other things have tended to obscure that Mysterion—the revelation of a God whose very nature is to give Self to Another, and who freely gives Self to creatures. The proper position of a theologian is as one prostrate before that Mystery. That also is the position of the Church Catholic in its life and liturgy. Like a jeweler holding a precious gem, we never tire of turning it about.

The Role of Theology

We can be consoled that the role of theology is perhaps not so much to say anything new, but, from out of the ambient of this world in which we live and the question it asks, to repeatedly attempt to glean some understanding into what is always new and refreshing:

- that Jesus of Nazareth lived and lives our humanity, died a death which is part of our lives, is raised up by God to whom he was obedient, because it was impossible that death should hold him;

- that in Jesus of Nazareth is revealed the Mystery hidden from all eternity . . . revealed precisely in our time (Hebrews 1, 1–4), in the tent of our flesh (John 1, 14);

- that it is into this Anointed One that we have been buried (Romans 6, 1–11) . . . so that we might know that through him, with him and in him all honor and glory is given to the Father by the power of the Spirit.

The proclamation of the victory of God, which is our hope, has occurred in our time and flesh in Jesus of Nazareth. God was faithful to Jesus even in death. The Anointed Jesus has given his Spirit to this Church—not the spirit of slavery to fall back into fear, but the Spirit which consoles (Romans 8). Nothing, *no thing*, can separate us from the Christ. Nothing.

Guided by the Spirit who sighs within us, we can say with confidence that when the Church GATHERS to proclaim the Mystery of Faith, its liturgy has everything to do with our journey toward human fulfillment.

Theology of the Liturgy is the systematic, often halting attempt to articulate what the Church does when it insists upon coming together to hear the Word and to break the Bread. But we base our reflection on the experience of faith—the encounter with the living Christ in our midst—out of which liturgical activity has sprung from the beginning, with *some contemporary situational comments:*

In a recent paper, Dr. Mark Searle has taken up the current questioning of infant baptism in the Catholic Tradition, especially with regard to the RCIA ("Infant Baptism in the Shadow of the RCIA"). He notes that, in his view, this question of the propriety of infant baptism is symptomatic of a more generalized crisis of belief in contemporary Catholicism. Changes in practice and shifts in doctrinal emphases prompted by Vatican II have led to a general uncertainty as to what it means to be a Catholic Christian in today's world.

Our own experiences of living through the twenty-plus years since the opening of the Council confirm Searle's point. Congregations of women have moved from relative certainty about what it means to be a religious community to literally questioning this form of commitment at all. These decades have seen a shift from considerable certainty about the meaning and content of the catechetical and educational projects, to a period of sometimes staggering confusion. Persons discerning vocation, like Jacob wrestling with the Angel of God (Genesis), struggle with what it means to be a Catholic, to belong to the Great Church. For essential to the 'Catholic thing' IS the Church, the Community.

Today, there are questions which were hardly ever asked before the Council: questions about the existence and meaning of original sin; the very value of inherited forms of belief and practice and the concomitant mistrust of authority and tradition; emphasis on individual freedom and self-determination in moral and religious matters; and last but not least, a long extant and profound lack of appreciation, even among practicing Catholics and clergy, of the riches of life lived before God in the *Ecclesia* of Christ in the power of the Spirit.

In the light of such observations, it seems somewhat audacious to speak of liturgy and human fulfillment in the same breath. Indeed, when Adrian Nocent began his now classic work, *The Liturgical Year*, he wondered whether the expression 'liturgical year' was not terribly outdated, and whether he might not be disturbing the dust on antiques in a museum, doors locked, inaccessible to the crowds of today's faithful. More importantly (he added in 1965) many do not see these celebrations as being in any way relevant to their life in the modern world (Intro., Vol. I).

This last point is haunting. We live in a country which discusses a 'permanent underclass' and in a world in which Christian armies massacre. At least eleven million people are jobless, and at least twenty million people go to bed hungry every night in the wealthiest country in the history of the world. International organizations of physicians and scientists show that the use of one nuclear weapon would most likely knock out all or most of the communications' capability on the planet, and that there would be no way of caring for those who might survive . . . and talk continues about the need for defense and closure of the weapons gap.

It is no simple matter, then, to say that the role of the theologian is to continually attempt to glean some insight into the Mystery of Christ's presence among us as celebrated in the Liturgy. Yet, this is exactly what we do here.

Spirituality

At least for purposes of discussion, let us describe spirituality as an immense phenomenon, the interior and exterior expression of one's experience of the Absolute, by whatever name. It is the result of the experience of 'relationship with' and of 'distinction from' the Nameless One. Further, spirituality—this interiorly and exteriorly expressed experience—is conditioned by the fact of one's identity, by all the factors which contribute to identity, above all by the experience of human relationships which, as human sciences tell us, begin before birth. So the point is that there is no purely 'individual' experience.

How is this universal phenomenon specified by the Christian experience of God?

Christian Spirituality

Imagine the following:

Jeremiah 31:31ff: See, the days are coming—it is Yahweh who speaks—when I will make a new covenant with the House of Israel . . . but not a covenant like the one I made with their ancestors . . . No, this is the covenant I will make with the House of Israel . . . Deep within them I will plant my law, writing it on their *hearts.*

1 Peter 3:8 & 15 ff: You should all agree among yourselves and be sympathetic; love the brothers (and sisters), have compassion and be self-effacing . . . reverence the Lord Christ in your hearts, and, always have your answer ready for people who ask you the reason for the hope that you have.

Philippians 1:19ff & 2:5–6: . . . thanks to your prayers and the help which will be given to me through the Spirit of Jesus . . . I shall never have to admit defeat, but now as always I shall have the courage for Christ to be glorified in my body, whether by my life or by my death.

In your minds you must be the same as Christ Jesus. His estate was divine, yet he did not cling to his equality with God . . .

Luke 24: That very same day, two of them were on their way to a village called Emmaus . . . Jesus himself came up and walked by their side . . . he said to them 'What matters are you discussing . . .?'

We know the story well. How Jesus explained the Scriptures to them, turning expectations upside down; how their hearts burned within them; how they recognized him in the breaking of the bread. If we heed the suggestion of Scripture scholars that this pericope is the first layer of the Gospel, then we can see that from the beginning, the ecclesia of the Lord has turned this jewel-meal round and round in its imagination, knowing that here it knows itself in the recognition of the Crucified-Risen Lord.

And if we say that the Gospel of John is the Gospel of the Body of the Lord *par excellence,* what might Chapter 6 demand? What might it mean to eat and drink the flesh and blood of the Lord? What might it mean to associate one's self with the flesh and the blood, or to have no life in us?

> *1 Corinthians 10:15–17:* The blessing-cup that we bless is a communion with the blood of Christ, and the bread that we break, is a communion with the body of Christ. The fact that there is only one loaf means that though there are many of us, we form a single body because we all have a share in this one loaf.

In Chapter 11 of First Corinthians, not 'recognizing the Body' (vs 29) refers to the selfishness with the less fortunate in the community.

What is to be made of Matthew's jarring injunction to first settle matters with the brothers and sisters and then to offer the sacrifice? And what could Augustine have intended by saying: See this Bread and this Cup and look upon *yourselves*?

These and so many more examples are richly ambiguous indications that in its 'imagination' the Ecclesia of Christ *knows* more than it can ever clearly philosophize about. It seems that in these lushly ambiguous statements we get some insight into the Christian experience of God which has from the beginning impelled the Church, not just to come together to hear the Word, but to eat a ritual meal together, to proclaim that the first Word of God is spoken in the community.

IMAGINATION—that capacity of human beings to integrate disparate information and to come to insight far beyond the conclusions of logic. The bits of insight referred to from Scripture lead, in the imagination of the Church to the following conclusion: *We cannot live without the Eucharist.*

We cannot nor could we ever exhaust this insight. But, a beginning effort can be made by considering two models for imagining the *activity of God in human history,* i.e., grace.

It isn't a question of opposing these models, because it would be wrong to say that they are experienced in opposition in the faith-imagination of the Church. But, their difference is rooted in the distinct manner in which the relation of God to the world is conceived.[1]

In the first position the activity of the Spirit in the world is regarded primarily as a spatially and temporally 'pointed interruption' of God into the world. The world is perceived as primarily and fundamentally *profane:* this is called 'nature' corrupted by original sin. If, therefore, the forgiving and divinizing grace of salvation (the self-communication of God) is to be given to the world, then, the Presence of the Spirit can only be conceived as entering or breaking into the world in separate, isolated moments. Recall the scholastic notion of 'actual grace.' If grace is given only at select moments *into* a profane and sinful world, then it must be seen as the *un-owed* gift from God—and, as Rahner has said, that seems to be the most that can be said about it.

From this perspective, the sacraments, the cultic or liturgical activity of the Church are seen as the temporal, moment-bound Events in which the Spirit is offered to a Spiritless or graceless world. The causality of the sacraments is understood as operating in a manner totally out of our control.

In this purview, grace always comes ever new 'from the outside' to the 'individual'—and it is difficult to see continuous historical and ecclesial expression. Fair enough. The sovereignty of God brooks no human control.

The second approach to understanding the operation of grace or the activity of the Spirit—and one which is continually being retrieved in post-Vatican II theology—proceeds from the conviction that the profane world is from the beginning pervaded and surrounded by the grace of *divine self-communication.* Hence, grace is understood as always and everywhere expressing itself in the world, either in the mode of pure gift to the freedom of an infant or to an adult. Even in rejection by sinners, the present Spirit judges and goads the heart. *The spirit is . . . always and everywhere.*

From this perspective, the un-owed-ness of the Spirit (from God's part) and the un-earned-ness (from our part) is not questioned. Rather, grace, the Spirit of the Father and of the Word, is always and everywhere the *given existential,* the truth, in the innermost core of human existence.

Hence, grace is not something secondary or added to nature as a kind of second-coming of God; rather, the Father is from the beginning loving and desirous of self-gift. (Recall the words of the eucharistic prayer: In love you created us . . . in mercy you redeemed us.) In this perspective, the dynamism of God, grace, the Spirit, is from the outset the ground of 'nature,' the inner core of this nature. For this reason, nature is not simply or purely profane; it is always seen as reconciled.

When personal freedom—always conditioned by human relationships—is exercised in the acceptance of the inner core of reality, this acceptance is the acceptance of God. These acceptances constitute salvation history. So, salvation history is not seen as being constituted by an ever new, moment-by-moment in-breaking of God into the profane world. Rather, this approach sees salvation history as the history of the divinization of the world. Salvation history is the history of THE GIVEN, so, in a true and radical sense, must be understood as the 'history of God'.

From this perspective, the sacraments, or cultic activity of the Church are not precisely seen as individual points in time of the inbreaking of God into the profane world; rather, the sacraments are seen as the outburst of the core-forever-Blessedness of the world, of the human community.

Today, in Catholic systematic theology, there is an increasing retrieval of a theology of creation within which we can situate this understanding of the communal liturgical activity of the Church and its radical implication: service of the brothers and sisters without distinction. Briefly, it proceeds in this way.

If all creation is the speaking forth of the Father in the One Logos or Word, and if, indeed, it participates in the being of the Word, then all creation is pleasing on the grounds of the personal relation of the Father to his Word in Love.[2]

And if we speak, as we do, of the relation between Father and Logos as the Spirit of Love, then it is clear that all creation is ordered, possessed, by the Spirit of Love.

According to this theology of creation, humanity knows that God is *for us*, that the coming forth of creation does not mean estrangement, but rather means the grounding of a 'with-one-another', the grounding of a radical community of God and creation in the Spirit. Here, there is no question of denying either the total sovereignty of God or the creaturehood of human beings. It is to deny that we are alone in the struggle. For if all creation is caught up in the Spirit, that is, in the Eternal Embrace of the Father and the Word, then even death cannot separate us. The Incarnation of the Word in the flesh of sin and death itself on the Cross makes this clear.

We can say that the *dialogue* of God and creation continues always . . . even when sin intervenes. The Mystery of redemption, thus, consists not in God's overlooking the deformity of sin, but in enduring it and accepting it in the flesh of sin through the Incarnate Word. So we can say that the Eternal Word obtains a *new historical presence* in Jesus Christ in our broken flesh, and that being conformed to the image of Jesus Christ does not simply mean being conformed to the Divine Logos. It means that human beings are to participate in the mystery of God revealed and realized in the Crucified One.

Let us linger a bit at this point. We say that creation is creation in the Logos, the Word, and that the new presence of the Word is in Jesus Christ. And as the Scriptures and *Sacrosanctum Concilium* repeat—it is the Crucified-Risen One who now sends the Spirit to the Church and thus to this world. The Spirit sent into our hearts, this new presence, cannot be separated from the Crucified-Risen One. It is this Spirit who, as John says, will teach us all we need to know. This Spirit of the Crucified One is the Source of the knowledge and efficacious power of the Church.

The 'two' on the road to Emmaus were stunned by the events in Jerusalem. They had great hopes that He was the one to redeem Israel . . . according to their plan. Just over twenty years ago the beloved Pope John began his inaugural address with the words "Gaudet mater ecclesia" (Mother Church rejoices). Now, twenty some years later we sometimes find ourselves in the shoes of the two on the road to Emmaus, stunned at the events which have dashed our hope—tempted to only look for the glorious events to discover the revelation of salvation, tempted to forget that the Spirit which quickens the Church is the Spirit of the Crucified One.

Looking back over these years, we too might be tempted to confusion and maybe to a degree of embarrassment. And so to us does the unrecognized Crucified Lord ask *the* rhetorical question:

> You slow of heart to believe! Was it not necessary that the Christ should suffer these things and *so* enter into his glory?
>
> *Sacrosanctum Concilium* #5 reads:
> For his humanity united with the Person of the Word was the instrument of salvation . . . it was from the side of Christ as he slept the sleep of death upon the Cross that there came forth "the wondrous sacrament of the whole Church."

Indeed, the Spirit given to us does not lead to a denial of the flesh. It does not escape the mire and confusion and pain and death. The Spirit leads the Church, the sacrament of salvation, in the fulfilling of the mission of Christ *here.*

In the viscera of the Church is the un-reflexive, preconceptual *knowledge* that having been embraced by the Spirit in virtue of Creation and in virtue of the Cross of Christ, we are not simply individuals, but radically with-one-another. Like Peter in John 6, we know there is really no place else to go.

Without such an approach it seems that any discussion of

the sacred liturgy and human fulfillment remains fragmented and embarrassed by the messiness of renewal.

Conclusion

In the sacred Liturgy we gather to celebrate the permanent presence of Christ by the power of the Spirit. But the Christ and his members cannot be separated. Thus, to eat and drink of the Lord is to partake of the Total Christ. It is to partake of the Incarnate Word of the Father who cannot be separated from the broken members of his Body.

This Mysterion is a shock to our world view. It turns our expectations upside down. We are asked to *imagine* that the utterly sovereign God is utterly Emmanuel, utterly and inseparably bound to this world of broken flesh.

This Mysterion is beyond our capacity to cognitively unpack. Witness the continual baulking of the early apocryphal gospels. These would have had Jesus be a marvelous Son of God who escapes the mire of this world. Recall also the Donatist controversy in which some said that only the rigorists could belong to the Church. These and others are expressions of the human mind's staggering at the *thought* that the Father has sent the Word into flesh which hungers and bleeds and makes mistakes.

If we say—and indeed we do—that THE experience of Christians is the experience of the utterly sovereign Word of God utterly related to our history and that the Spirit of Christ *dwells* in us, binding us together; if we say that that experience is on-going, now, in the Body which cannot be separated from its Head; and if we say that the Meal was and is the place wherein we recognize him who explains us to ourselves—and that it was from out of these gatherings that the very gospels grew—*Then* the words of SC, #2 explode:

> The Liturgy daily builds up those who are in the Church, making of them a holy temple of the Lord, a dwelling place for God in the Spirit, to the mature measure of the fullness of Christ.

The Great Church has always had to say that from the perspective of God, the sacraments are not necessary for salvation. But the Christian experience of the gift of the Spirit to the Church impels the Church to gather . . . and especially to come to the Table, because the Spirit teaches us that *there* it has most clearly been taught who God is and where God dwells.

Finally, and painfully so, there seems to be, even among practicing Catholics and clergy, a profound lack of appreciation of this glorious and earthy 'Catholic thing'. But given *the given*, we look upon these times as another bout of wrestling with the Angel of God. You see, when Jacob finished wrestling, he asked the angel, "What is your Name?" The Scriptures then read: "*and there the angel blessed him*" (Genesis 32, 24–29).

NOTES

1. Karl Rahner, "Zur Theologie des Gottesdienstes," *Theologische Quartalschrift* 159 (1979) 162–169.

2. Raphael Schulte, "Die Einzelsakramente als Ausgliederung des Wurzelsakramentes," in *Mysterium Salutis*, Vol. 4/2. *Das Heilsgeschehen in der Gemeinde. Gottes Gnaden-Handeln.* Einsiedeln-Zurich-Cologne: Benziger, 1973, pp. 46–151.

About the Authors

CARL A. LAST is Director of Continuing Education for the Archdiocese of Milwaukee. An experienced teacher and lecturer, Father Last is on the Board of Directors of the National Organization for Continuing Education of Roman Catholic Clergy and a member of the North American Academy of Liturgy. He holds an M. Div. from St. Francis Seminary in Milwaukee and an M.A. in Liturgical Studies from the University of Notre Dame. The co-author of *Take and Eat*, the national catechesis of Communion in the hand, he has also written a series of parish vesper services published by FDLC.

REV. ANSCAR J. CHUPUNGCO, O.S.B. is a monk of the Benedictine Abbey of Our Lady of Montserrat in Manila. Since 1978 he has served as President of the Pontifical Liturgical Institute, Rome, where he is also a professor of History of Liturgy and Principles of Liturgical Adaptation. Father Chupungco is Consultor to the Sacred Congregation for Divine Worship, and author of *Cultural Adaptation of the Liturgy* (Paulist Press), *Toward a Filipino Liturgy, Cosmic Elements of Christian Passover*, and several articles on liturgical adaptation.

REV. EDWARD J. KILMARTIN, S.J. has served as Professor of Theology at the University of Notre Dame since 1975. He was a professor of theology for 16 years at the Weston School of Theology, Cambridge, Massachusetts and served as visiting professor at the Melbourne, Australia Theology Complex and at the University of San Francisco. Father Kilmartin is the author of *Church, Christ and Priesthood* (Paulist Press) and *The Eucharist in the Primitive Church* as well as more than thirty articles in the areas of literary criticism of New Testament sources, the history of theology and systematic theology.

THERESA F. KOERNKE, I.H.M. is a sister of the Immaculate Heart of Mary, Monroe, Michigan. She is currently a candidate for a Ph.D. in Theology at the University of Notre Dame. She holds M.A.s in English and American Literature and in New Testament Studies/Systematics from the University of Detroit. Sister Theresa is a member of The North American Academy of Liturgy and The American Academy of Religion and has been published in *Assembly* and in *Understanding the Sunday Readings,* Commentary and Study Guide.

REV. MSGR. FREDERICK R. McMANUS is Vice Provost and Dean of Graduate Studies and Professor of Canon Law at The Catholic University of America. Father McManus served as Consultant to the Pontifical Preparatory Commission on Sacred Liturgy (1960–62) and was a Peritus, II Vatican Council. He is a staff consultant to the NCCB's Committee on Liturgy where he served as Director of the Secretariat for ten years. His many books include *The Ceremonies of the Easter Vigil, Handbook for the New Rubrics, The Rite of Penance,* and *Sacramental Liturgy.* In addition he is editor of *The Jurist* and a regular contributor to professional liturgical and canonical journals.

REV. KEVIN SEASOLTZ, O.S.B. is a Benedictine monk of St. Anselm's Abbey, Washington, D.C. and a Professor in the School of Religious Studies at The Catholic University of America. He is also an adjunct professor of Theology at St. John's University, Collegeville, Minnesota and serves on the editorial boards of *Worship* and *Social Thought.* His professional membership includes The North American Academy of Liturgy, Catholic Theological Society of America, and Canon Law Society of America. Father Seasoltz's recent publications include *New Liturgy, New Law, Living Bread, Saving Cup,* plus contributions to *Worship, Clergy Review* and *Concilium.*